The School Leader's Guide to
Grading

KEN O'CONNOR

A Joint Publication

Copyright © 2013 by Solution Tree Press

All rights reserved, including the right of reproduction of this book in whole or in part in any form.

Essentials for Principals is a registered trademark of the National Association of Elementary School Principals.

555 North Morton Street
Bloomington, IN 47404
800.733.6786 (toll free) / 812.336.7700
FAX: 812.336.7790

email: info@solution-tree.com
solution-tree.com

Printed in the United States of America

16 15 14 13 12   1 2 3 4 5

Library of Congress Cataloging-in-Publication Data

O'Connor, Ken.
   The school leader's guide to grading / Ken O'Connor.
      pages cm
   Includes bibliographical references and index.
   ISBN 978-1-935542-52-0 (perfect bound) 1. Grading and marking (Students) 2. Educational leadership. 3. School administrators--Handbooks, manuals, etc. I. Title.
   LB3060.37.O275 2013
   371.27'2--dc23
                         2012039887

Solution Tree

Jeffrey C. Jones, CEO
Edmund M. Ackerman, President

Solution Tree Press

President: Douglas M. Rife
Publisher: Robert D. Clouse
Editorial Director: Lesley Bolton
Managing Production Editor: Caroline Wise
Senior Production Editor: Edward Levy
Proofreader: Rachel Rosolina
Text Designer: Jenn Taylor
Text Compositor: Amy Shock
Cover Designers: Orlando Angel and Amy Shock

To my wife, Marilyn, who has supported, encouraged, loved, and put up with me for over forty years.

ACKNOWLEDGMENTS

Since 1995, I have been able to focus my professional learning on grading and reporting, and it is important that I acknowledge the people from whom I have learned most. The experts include Susan Brookhart, Damian Cooper, Jan Chappuis, Steve Chappuis, Tom Guskey, Jay McTighe, Douglas Reeves, Rick Stiggins, Ruth Sutton, Dylan Wiliam, Rick Wormeli, and Alison Zmuda. I have also had the good fortune to work in many schools and districts and the privilege of learning from and with a number of educators, including Sarah Craig, Myron Dueck, Terri Durgan, Rosemary Evans, Danny Hill, Becca Lindahl, Hugh O'Donnell, Melissa Thompson, Tom Schimmer, Janna Smith, and Dale Skoreyko.

I have also benefited from my association with PowerSchool and have learned from Chris Alldredge, Paul Smith, and Danny Zeibert. I am very impressed with the approaches to standards-based grading and reporting done by the following schools and school districts: American School of Doha, Qatar; Branksome Hall, Toronto; Bremerton School District, Washington; Caesar Rodney School District, Delaware; Danville Schools, Michigan; Halifax Regional School Board, Nova Scotia; Jakarta International School, Indonesia; Lawrence Public Schools, Kansas; Limestone District School Board, Ontario; Lincoln Public Schools, Nebraska; Minnetonka High School, Minnesota; Ottawa-Carleton District School Board, Ontario; Prairie South School Division, Saskatchewan; Quakertown Community School District, Pennsylvania; St. Michaels University School, British Columbia; Urbana City Schools, Ohio; and Westside Community Schools, Nebraska.

I would like to express my appreciation to all those individuals and organizations that gave me permission to include their material in this book. I must also acknowledge the assistance I received in gathering materials from Sarah Craig, Terri Durgan, Leslie Lukin, Glenda Nouskhajian, Gail Seay, and Lendy Willis.

I would also like to express my appreciation to Douglas Rife for seeing the need for this topic in the series and for inviting me to write it. I also would like to thank the editor, Ed Levy, and the designer, Amy Shock, for their considerable help in crafting the final product. As the author, I take full responsibility for the ideas in the book, but the final product has been improved immeasurably by the contributions of many other professionals. I also express my gratitude to the thousands of teachers who have attended my workshops, from whom I have learned so much.

—Ken O'Connor

Solution Tree Press would like to acknowledge the following reviewers:

Sharon Brighton
Principal
Sodt Elementary School
Monroe, Minnesota

Michelle Cruckshank
Principal
Waller Road Elementary School
Tacoma, Washington

Dawn Hagness
Northeastern Nevada Regional Professional
    Development Program
Elko, Nevada

Dana Harris
Principal
Ridgecrest Elementary School
Puyallup, Washington

Seth Kennard
Principal
Charles Barrett Elementary School
Alexandria, Virginia

Tim Lowe
Principal
Grace Jordan Elementary School
Boise, Idaho

Toby Melver
Principal
Northside Elementary School
Elko, Nevada

Will Remmert
Principal
Washington and Jefferson Elementary Schools
Mankato, Minnesota

Rosalyn Rice-Harris
Principal
Jefferson-Houston School
Alexandria, Virginia

TABLE OF CONTENTS

ABOUT THE AUTHOR

Ken O'Connor is an independent consultant specializing in grading and reporting. He has been a staff-development presenter and facilitator in the United States and Canada and in fifteen countries outside North America. Ken's thirty-three-year teaching career includes experience as a geography teacher, department head, and curriculum coordinator responsible for student assessment and evaluation. He has also served as a consultant on secondary assessment to the Ontario Ministry of Education.

Ken's articles have appeared in the *NASSP Bulletin*, *Educational Leadership*, and *Orbit*. He is author of two previous books, *How to Grade for Learning, K–12* and *A Repair Kit for Grading: 15 Fixes for Broken Grades*.

Ken is husband to Marilyn, with whom he celebrated his fortieth wedding anniversary in 2012, father to Jeremy and Bronwyn, and grandfather to twins Elliot and Vivian.

A sports fanatic, he has been involved in the administration of field hockey as well as umpiring and playing. He was umpire for men's field hockey matches at the 1984 Olympic Games and at the 1990 World Cup. More recently, he has become a very keen golfer and has particularly enjoyed playing Pebble Beach in California, Bandon Dunes in Oregon, Whistling Straits in Wisconsin, and the Old Course at St. Andrews in Scotland.

Visit www.oconnorgrading.com to learn more about Ken's work. To book Ken for professional development, contact pd@solution-tree.com.

PREFACE

This book is intended to provide principals with ideas that will improve their effectiveness in helping and supporting their teachers in evaluating and communicating student achievement. It is also intended to provide principals with knowledge that will help them meet the standards of the National Association of Elementary School Principals (NAESP), as outlined in the second edition of *Leading Learning Communities: Standards for What Principals Should Know and Be Able to Do* (National Association of Elementary School Principals, 2002). To varying degrees, this book addresses all of the standards, with a particular emphasis on Standard 5: "Manage data and knowledge to inform decisions and measure progress of student, adult, and school performance" (National Association of Elementary School Principals, 2002, p. 9).

The School Leader's Guide to Grading presents a summary and reorientation of the ideas in my two previous books, *A Repair Kit for Grading* and *How to Grade for Learning*.

I have included samples of policies and procedures from schools and school districts that principals will find useful. I would like to express my appreciation to all of those who gave me permission to use their materials. I would also like it to be clear that the samples are *examples*, not models, and that while all have strong features, some have weaknesses. If you like them, you should not simply adopt them—you should *adapt* them for your situation.

The book consists of an introduction, four chapters on how principals can make grading effective and educative in their schools, a conclusion, and four appendices.

The introduction identifies some of the essentials of grading. It defines the key terms, raises the "essential question," identifies the four critical conditions for effective grades, and enumerates "the seven Ps" that interact to produce what actually happens in schools and classrooms during the assessment and grading process. Since principals are themselves one of the seven Ps, the role of the principal is highlighted throughout the discussion.

Chapter 1 reaffirms that school is about learning, not the accumulation of points, and shows how principals can honor and emphasize learning in the assessment and grading process in their schools. Chapter 2 describes what is essential for principals to be aware of and monitor to ensure that grades are accurate. Chapter 3 provides information about why assessment and grading must be standards based and what principals need to know to help their teachers effectively implement standards-based grading. Chapter 4 is about consistency, which comes from clear, criterion-referenced performance standards and from policy and procedures that require shared practices among the teachers in the school and district. The conclusion states what must be done to move forward with grading in standards-based schools in the 21st century. The appendices include sample policies and school district report cards.

INTRODUCTION

In a perfect world there would be no grades—at least, not as we know them now.

—Susan M. Brookhart

Grading, as I use the term in this book, refers to the use of symbols—letters or numbers—to summarize student achievement over a stated period of time. It is important to note that grades are different from "marking" or "scoring," which refer to the symbols used to represent student achievement on each individual piece of assessment evidence.

Grades have been a fixture in North American schools for over one hundred years, and despite many criticisms, their use continues because of state, district, and school policies and community expectations. There have been many calls for reform, and while there has been significant change in the early elementary grades in many schools, grading has been remarkably impervious to change in upper elementary and middle schools. As the quote from Brookhart (2009) suggests, grades, while not ideal, can be made more acceptable. This means that principals should look critically at the grading and assessment procedures used in their schools. If those procedures are not in the best interests of students, principals should advocate a process that leads to change. This, however, is a difficult task, because as Joseph Brown (2004) has noted, "teachers are very sensitive about their grading practices—they regard them as sacred ground" (p. 29). Moreover, it is also important to take into account the views of parents and students in the grading process, so principals must provide avenues for their input as well.

Before proceeding further, it is necessary to have a clear explanation of the key terms and concepts used in this book.

The Essential Question

In *Understanding by Design*, the book that describes their approach to curriculum design, Grant Wiggins and Jay McTighe (2005) demonstrate the huge value that essential questions have in planning curriculum, instruction, and assessment. Essential questions are those that are absolutely necessary to ask. To identify and support effective grading in their schools, principals must frequently raise and seek to answer positively this essential question: How confident are we that the grades students receive and the grading procedures we use in our school are (1) supportive of learning,

(2) accurate, (3) meaningful, and (4) consistent? These represent the essential conditions of quality for effective grading.

Grades Must Be Supportive of Learning

[handwritten margin note: Purpose of School - learning]

Above all, grades must be supportive of learning; all stakeholders need to understand that a school's core mission is learning for all. This requires understanding, first that learning is a process that is often initially unsuccessful, and early learning difficulties should not be held against students; and second that most learning, especially at the elementary level, is cumulative and developmental, and what matters most is the more recent achievement. This is why not everything students do should be scored, and everything that is scored should not have equal weight in the final determination of a grade. Such an approach is very different from traditional grading practice, in which teachers put a score on almost everything that students do, and every score is part of the determination of grades. Principals have to lead the way, so that everyone involved understands and supports learning. Put another way, everyone involved must see school as a learning game, not a grading game.

Grades Must Be Accurate

Grades must be accurate, because very important decisions—about and by students—are made based on grades. Unfortunately, traditional grading has often been inaccurate as a result of three common practices:

[handwritten margin note: Common practices of inaccurate grades]

1. Mixing achievement and behavior together in the determination of grades

2. Using inappropriate, often mathematically incorrect, calculations to determine grades

3. Determining grades based on assessments of varying and often low quality

Principals should assist teachers in becoming quality assessors who use their professional judgment, not just calculations, to produce grades that accurately summarize achievement.

Grades Must Be Meaningful

Grades must be meaningful. Putting a letter or number symbol on a report card to summarize student achievement in a subject has little meaning by itself. Getting a B in history tells students and parents almost nothing about what a student is good at and what needs improvement. To be meaningful, grades need to be based on standards, outcomes, or expectations—or whatever learning goals are called in your school or district. Where standards are in place, teachers can explain which aspects of learning are strong and which need improvement, and they can also point to specific strategies that will help. To be truly meaningful, therefore, grades should be provided not for subjects but for standards—that is, students should receive a grade not for mathematics but for specific math skills and for the understanding of specific math concepts. Instead of a C for math, for example, the report card would show that a student is excelling in calculation and estimation and is proficient in measurement and geometry but has limited understanding of fractions and problem solving. Principals should guide teachers to provide such profiles of student achievement, which give information that can be used to help students achieve at higher levels in the future.

Grades Must Be Consistent

Finally, grades must be consistent. A grade should not depend on whether students are in teacher X's or teacher Y's class; students who are achieving at the same level should get the same grade. All too often, this has not been the case. In almost every school, some teachers have been identified as "hard," and other teachers have been identified as "soft" or "easy." This happens because most teachers have had little opportunity to learn about grading in their pre- or in-service training, so they grade the way they were graded as students or according to the way they were mentored early in their careers. Principals have a critical role to play in moving grading from an individual, idiosyncratic activity to a shared practice based on agreed-on principles and procedures. They need to find ways to provide teams of teachers with the time to engage in professional dialogue about grading and in shared marking of student assessments.

The Seven Ps

Ultimately, the *procedures* that teachers are expected or required to use determine whether grades will meet the conditions of quality described in the previous section. These procedures are the result of the interaction of six other factors—*purpose, principles, practices, policy, practicality,* and *principals.*

Some of the primary ways that these seven Ps interact are indicated in figure I.1.

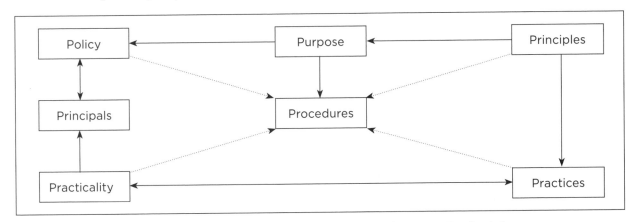

Source: Created by Ken O'Connor. Artwork developed by Heidi Bay, Grey Sky Design, Portland, Oregon.

Figure I.1: The seven Ps of grading.

Procedures

District or school regulations should be outlined as procedures in public, published formats—for example, on the district or school website. In the past, procedures have often been very limited in scope and in some cases have not existed at all. Increasingly, however, schools and districts have realized that for grading to be effective, procedures that all teachers use need to be in place. Such procedures are often developed by a committee or task force that includes representatives of the school or district administration and classroom teachers. Some schools and districts include parents and students on these committees.

Procedures are often derived from policy—broad statements of general intent—and then set out as administrative regulations—with details that identify specifics. For example, the Des Moines Independent Community School District describes the interplay between policy and procedure as follows:

> Board policy shall establish the general direction for what the District seeks to accomplish. The superintendent shall be responsible for the implementation of board policy through administrative policies and procedures. Policies may be proposed by any member of the Board, by school district personnel, or by any citizen or group of citizens in the school district. It shall be the responsibility of the superintendent or his/her designee to establish an Administrative Policy/Procedure Committee to review policies at least every five years to ensure compliance with Iowa law. Board member representation on the committee is required. Administrative policies and procedures, which implement the policies of the Board, may be developed by the superintendent and reviewed by the Administrative Policy/Procedure Committee. The Board shall approve new or revised administrative policies to the extent required by law. The Board shall be notified of all other new or revised administrative policies and procedures. (Des Moines Public Schools, n.d.a)

Purpose

What we see as the purpose of grading is affected by, and affects, a number of the other Ps, both directly and indirectly. If we think logically when we have difficulty deciding what to do, we go back to purpose, and like a compass, that will usually point us in a clear direction. It is therefore essential that schools and districts possess a shared understanding of the primary purpose of grades.

Grades have traditionally served a number of purposes, including communication of student learning, self-evaluation, selection and sorting of students, motivation, and program evaluation (Guskey, 1996). Depending on which of these purposes they regard as primary, teachers will determine grades in different ways. Middle School Principal Joseph Brown (2004) asks, "If educators differ on what grades represent, what are parents supposed to think or understand?" (p. 30). He further notes that "it is even more confusing to parents whose children have six, seven, or eight teachers, each of whom has their own grading philosophy" (Brown, 2004, p. 30). Brown (2004) believes that there is value in teachers coming together as a faculty and answering the question of why they grade students, because "by reflecting on the research and sharing in an open discussion with their peers, faculty members can become more confident in their grading practice and have more confidence in what the grade represents" (p. 30). Brookhart (2011) suggests that in the professional dialogue about grading, "the important thing is to examine beliefs and assumptions about the meaning and purpose of grades *first*" (p. 12, emphasis mine).

The premise on which the rest of this book rests, and what guides me when considering difficult issues about grading, is my agreement with Jane M. Bailey and Jay McTighe (1996) that the primary purpose of grades is "to *communicate student achievement* to students, parents, school administrators, post-secondary institutions and employers" (p. 120, emphasis mine).

Whether or not you agree, it is essential that there be dialogue in your school and district that results in a shared understanding of the primary purpose of grades and that this shared understanding be published and accessible to all stakeholders.

Principles

Principles are the set of values that orient and rule the conduct of an individual or an organization. In the field of education, these values have a huge impact on what individuals or organizations believe should be the procedures for grading.

In education, there are principles of quality instruction, assessment, and communication that individuals and institutions acknowledge and try to put into practice. Ideally, principles are the basis for policy, but sometimes there is tension between them. It is therefore essential as principals examine (and consider making changes to) teachers' grading and reporting procedures that they be clear about the policies they are required to put in place and the principles they would like to make come alive in their schools. These principles will come alive through the purpose teachers establish for grades, the procedures they are required to use, and the practices they follow in their classrooms and gradebooks.

An example of a set of educational principles can be found in *Principles of Learning and Teaching P–12 and Their Components*, developed by the Department of Education and Early Childhood Development (2009) of Victoria, Australia. These principles state that students learn best when:

- The learning environment is supportive and productive
- The learning environment promotes independence, interdependence and self motivation
- Students' needs, backgrounds, perspectives and interests are reflected in the learning program
- Students are challenged and supported to develop deep levels of thinking and application
- Assessment practices are an integral part of teaching and learning
- Learning connects strongly with communities and practice beyond the classroom.

With regard specifically to principles of assessment (of which grading is a part), the Assessment Reform Group (2002) in the United Kingdom has done some of the best research in the world. According to their principles, assessment:

- Is part of effective planning
- Focuses on how students learn
- Is central to classroom practice
- Is a key professional skill
- Is sensitive and constructive

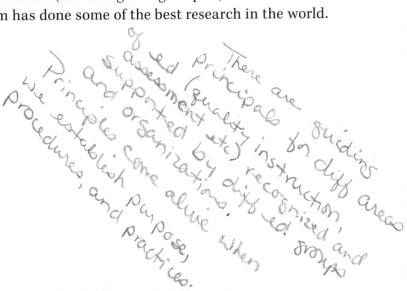

- Fosters motivation

- Promotes understanding of goals and criteria

- Helps learners know how to improve

- Develops the capacity for self-assessment [and peer assessment]

- Recognizes all educational achievement

These principles of assessment from Bay District Schools (2010) in Florida help us see how principles of assessment translate to the district level:

1. The primary purpose of assessment is to improve learning for all students.

2. Assessment is aligned to standards.

3. A quality assessment plan supported by best practices in research should facilitate learning.

4. Grading is fair, consistent, and meaningful.

5. Communication regarding student achievement is timely, ongoing, and aligned to standards.

6. Roles and responsibilities are clearly defined, communicated, and understood by all.

Implementing principles like these can provide a significant challenge for principals. Often, they are reflected in the school mission or vision statement. An example of such a statement is the pledge developed at Lexington County School District One, in Lexington, South Carolina (Lexington County School District One, n.d.)

> The mission of Lexington County School District One—where caring people, academics, the arts and athletics connect—is to prepare 21st century graduates while serving as the center for community learning.
>
> Therefore, we will provide:
>
> - An array of exceptional learning experiences in a high-performance culture of excellence that sets high expectations for every student
>
> - Opportunities to develop talents, interests and skills through choices from a comprehensive system of 21st century learning experiences in the arts, academics and athletics
>
> - Various innovative learning delivery and support systems to personalize learning and to ensure that our students are learning sophisticated 21st century skills, knowledge and attitudes
>
> - Opportunities to practice leadership and citizenship in a global context
>
> - Access by the community to a range of learning and participatory community experiences throughout life
>
> - A learning environment and professional culture of caring and support

[Handwritten margin notes: "3 areas Prins need to address / Judgment / motivation / fairness", "by Practices determined -or- by beliefs determined", "beliefs determined -or- by Prac"]

Practices

There is disagreement about whether the practices teachers put in place in their classrooms are determined by their beliefs or whether their beliefs are determined by their practices. It is clear, however, that in a number of important aspects, the practices and beliefs of teachers affect how they conduct assessment, grading, and reporting. I believe there are three key areas in which principals must engage their faculties in professional dialogue to support them in becoming reflective practitioners, developing beliefs, and putting in place practices that support learning for all students. These three key aspects are (1) professional judgment, (2) motivation, and (3) fairness.

Professional Judgment

Grading has traditionally been seen simply as an exercise in averaging the scores from whatever items teachers decided to count toward the grade. This was regarded as appropriate because it made grading appear to be objective. But this not only reduces the teacher's role to that of mere number cruncher or bookkeeper, it is also a distorted notion of grading. Teachers have always claimed to be, and want to be seen as, professional; part of being professional is having craft or specialized knowledge and using that knowledge to make decisions. To be professional in grading, teachers must do more than simply crunch numbers; they must use numbers to inform but not determine their decisions. One reason for this is that the assessment and grading process is, to a considerable extent, subjective; assessments arise from teachers' subjective (professional) decisions about what to include in the assessment and their subjective judgment about the level of performance of each student on the assessment.

Teachers should not apologize for being subjective, and principals should support them in developing confidence in their professional judgment. However, they need to be clear that professional judgment does not mean people doing "their own thing"; rather, it means striving for consistency through shared understanding of purpose and policy and through agreement on the principles every teacher is striving to put into practice. Principals should encourage dialogue about what is— and what is not—professional judgment. This is why Damian Cooper (2011) defines professional judgment as "decisions made by educators, in light of experience, and with reference to shared public standards and established policies and guidelines" (p. 3).

Motivation

Traditionally, teachers, parents, and especially grandparents have believed that grades are effective and appropriate motivators for students—the promise of good grades (and the extra rewards that result) and the threat of bad grades (and all the negatives that come with them) were believed to cause students to work hard and behave well. As a result, the motivational practices of teachers have often made it appear that school was not about learning but about the accumulation of points. Many teachers have established reward systems in which students' grades were directly or indirectly inflated by good behaviors and deflated by what were deemed to be bad behaviors. Systems like these that emphasize extrinsic motivation may work with some students—those who do well—but they certainly don't work for all students. According to Alfie Kohn (2011), research has demonstrated that extrinsic rewards frequently have a negative impact on learning and that

[Handwritten margin note: "focus on grades, not learning"]

"grades tend to diminish students' interest in whatever they are learning, . . . create a preference for the easiest possible task, . . . and tend to reduce the quality of students' thinking" (pp. 29–30).

My visits to elementary classrooms show teachers frequently using extrinsic motivational practices—emphasizing the importance of grades and using them along with gold stars, stickers, and points as the carrot or the stick. Teachers need to be made aware of modern research into motivation and provided with opportunities to reflect on and discuss their grading practices.

Daniel Pink (2009) makes a very convincing case that the motivational environment we should be promoting is intrinsic motivation, what he calls "Motivation 3.0." Here, the main motivators are:

1. The freedom to (sometimes) do what you want to do, how you want to do it

2. The opportunity to take a challenge and get better and better

3. The fulfillment that comes from understanding how what you are doing will help you and others

He comes to this conclusion by studying modern psychological research into motivation and by looking at companies that have been very successful using nontraditional approaches. Pink suggests that there are three keys to Motivation 3.0—*autonomy*, *mastery*, and *purpose*. This has huge implications for the practices teachers use in their classrooms.

Autonomy means that teachers should include in their classroom practices, as frequently as feasible, opportunities for students to choose how they learn, how they show they have learned, and, at times, what they are learning.

Mastery, according to Pink (2009), is not necessarily a high level of achievement; it is seeing oneself getting better, because that is when people are willing to continue to try. When they cannot see how they are doing or when they see no hope of getting better, they give up. This means teachers must ensure that students can (age-appropriately) clearly see the learning goals—both the "what" and the "how well"—and that they can self-assess their learning. The ability to self-assess is critical to all learning, whether one is young or old, but self-assessment is a learned skill. Teachers must help students by providing them with many opportunities to self- and peer-assess, feedback on the quality of their self-assessment, and guidance on how to improve.

Clarity of *purpose* is necessary because we are much more likely to be engaged in any task for which the relevance and usefulness is understood.

It is my experience that most teachers have had very little opportunity for professional learning or dialogue about motivation, so it is important that principals include motivation in the professional learning opportunities for their faculty. Authors who have useful ideas about motivation for teachers to study and discuss include Pink (2009), Carol Dweck (2006), Marvin Marshall (2007, 2012), Bob Sullo (2009), and Judy Willis (2006). I particularly recommend Marvin Marshall's monthly

Promoting Responsibility and Learning newsletter. It is free, and it always has sections on promoting responsibility, increasing effectiveness, improving relationships, and advancing learning. The newsletter can be obtained by entering your email address at www.marvinmarshall.com in the yellow newsletter box.

Fairness

Teacher practices and beliefs about fairness have a huge impact on what happens in the classroom, especially in the areas of assessment and grading, so this is another topic that principals should include in the professional learning plan for their schools.

Traditionally in schools, fairness has been seen as identical to uniformity—we are fair when we treat all students in the same way—for example, in the application of school rules and by having all students do the same assessment in the same amount of time. But students are not all the same, so to treat them in the same way is actually unfair. We don't say that either all students or no students can wear glasses; we differentiate, and only students who need them wear glasses. In other words, we allow for equal opportunity for all students to be able to see clearly what they need to see in the classroom. This same principle should apply to everything that happens in the classroom. Fairness is not uniformity; fairness is equal opportunity. This means that teachers must know their students well and be able to adapt learning opportunities and assessments so that all students have an equal opportunity to learn, to demonstrate their learning, and to earn grades that accurately communicate their level of achievement.

Policy

Policy has legal or quasi-legal status in schools and must be followed by employees. The responsibilities of principals include ensuring that their staff is familiar with relevant policies and monitoring compliance with those policies. Principals also need to develop school policies and must ensure that they are not in conflict with state and district policies, because policies exist within the nested hierarchy shown in figure I.2 (page 10). State policies are usually broad and general and set the limits for policy at other levels. District policies are usually a little more specific but still fairly broad and general. The state and district levels set the limits for school policies that are even more specific, and for procedures that are often very specific. An example for a school district can be found in appendix A, and an example for a school within that district can be found in appendix B. Within the limits set by the other levels, teachers should develop the procedures that will be used in their classrooms and make them available for administrators and parents. An example of a teacher-classroom policy can be found in chapter 4.

Policy should be based on principles, but at the state and district levels politics often has a considerable influence, resulting occasionally in tension between policy and principle. It is therefore essential that all involved, especially principals, know the policies they must abide by and the principles they value and would like to implement.

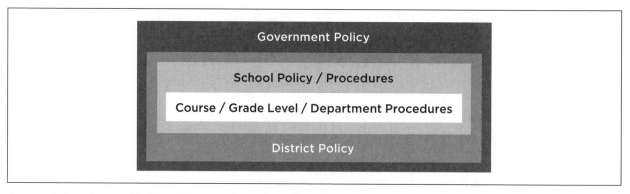

Source: Original created by Ken O'Connor. Artwork developed by Heidi Bay, Grey Sky Design, Portland, Oregon.

Figure I.2: The nested hierarchy of policy and procedures.

Practicality

Policies are made and principles are stated, but the processes of teaching, learning, and communicating have to actually work in schools and classrooms, so they have to be practical. The way policies and principles are implemented may look a little different in kindergarten compared to fourth grade compared to eighth grade, and they may look a little different in English than in physical education and science. In other words, we often make small adaptations to policy and principles by following the spirit of the policy and principles but not all the details.

As an example of how practicality modifies principles, there is a widely accepted principle of quality assessment that getting an accurate summary of student achievement in a grade needs to be based on a variety of assessment evidence, ideally evidence gathered from writing, observation and performance, and oral communication and conversation. However, in kindergarten and early elementary grades, there is more emphasis on observation and conversation because of limited ability with writing, while in high school there is more emphasis on writing because of the larger number of students with whom each teacher interacts. The proportion of evidence from each source also varies with the nature of the subject—for example, there is more written evidence in English language arts and more performance evidence in physical education and drama classes.

Principals

It is well established that the actions of principals have a huge impact on how well schools operate and on the quality of teaching and student achievement in each school (DuFour & Marzano, 2011). It is also essential that principals provide informed leadership for the communication of learning in their school. Principals must ensure that their teachers have a shared understanding of:

- The primary purpose of grades

- The policies they are required to implement

- The principles they want to operationalize

- The importance of being reflective practitioners

- The meaning and appropriate use of professional judgment

- Fairness as equal opportunity

Principals must also provide opportunities for ongoing professional learning, especially about motivation, grading, and reporting. They must monitor implementation of state and district policies and develop school policy and procedures. Principals should also provide guidance to their teachers in the development of grade-level and course procedures. These procedures should be consistent for teachers who are teaching the same grade level or course. If there is more than one teacher teaching a grade level or a course in a school, the principal must ensure that these teachers have opportunities to meet to develop and then review and revise those procedures.

There is a nasty little four-letter word for what is required for all of this—*time*—and I believe that one of the key roles for principals in 21st century schools is to be creative in finding ways for teachers to have time for professional dialogue and collaboration. Sometimes this should occur in small groups like grade-level or subject teams, but there are many times when all the teachers in a school need to be hearing the same things and be part of schoolwide professional learning and dialogue.

[handwritten margin note: time — some small group but other time whole staff]

Summary

In this introduction, I have identified some of the essentials of grading. I defined the key terms, raised the essential question, identified the four critical conditions for grades to be effective, and identified the seven Ps that interact to produce what actually happens in schools and classrooms during the assessment and grading process. Principals are one of the seven Ps, and throughout the discussion of the Ps, I highlighted the role that principals should play.

CHAPTER 1

Grading That Supports Learning

From a very early age, students get the message that school is about grades and all that matters is that they get good grades. This chapter turns that model on its head and focuses instead on how grading can support learning.

Students and parents who believe school is just about grades focus inevitably on the accumulation of points. This orientation is revealed very clearly by the question that students and parents always ask teachers—What can I do to improve my grade?—when the question they should be asking is, What can I do to improve my learning?

Of course, one way that principals can get their teachers and students focused on learning, not grades, is to eliminate grades altogether. Although a tiny minority of schools has already done that, in most schools grades are inescapable because of state or district policy and community and parental expectations.

If grades in some form are inevitable, what can principals do to keep the focus on learning? First, they can ensure that all concerned understand that learning is the core purpose of their school. Second, they can ensure that the learning process is honored in the school's assessment and grading procedures. There must also be a clear understanding that grades are determined primarily from summative assessments and that when learning is cumulative and developmental only the more recent evidence is used to determine grades.

Learning as the Core Purpose

To assist small rural school districts in Manitoba, Canada in successfully implementing new report cards, the Manitoba Rural Learning Consortium developed the diagram in figure 1.1 (page 14), which functions as an organizer for thinking about teaching for learning. There are a number of notable aspects to the diagram. The top half is focused on learning in three steps—(1) defining learning goals, (2) planning for learning, and (3) teaching for learning—while the bottom half is focused on the use of assessment to move the teaching and learning process forward. The diagram shows that teaching for learning is a process that starts with defining learning goals and proceeds through planning and teaching for learning to the gathering of assessment information, which is then used to adjust teaching and learning. It also shows that those in leadership roles should use their roles

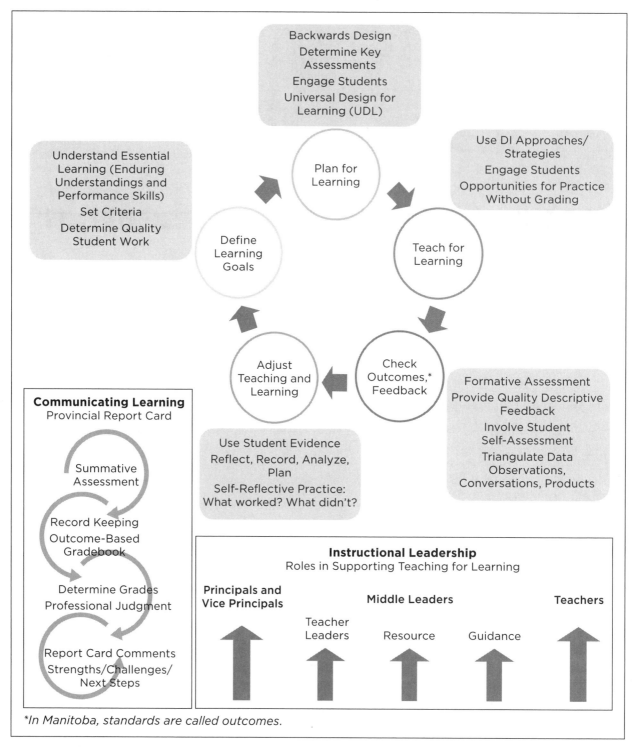

In Manitoba, standards are called outcomes.

Source: Manitoba Rural Learning Consortium, Manitoba, Canada. Used with permission.

Figure 1.1: Manitoba Rural Learning Consortium teaching-for-learning diagram.

to support teaching and assessing for learning. The diagram clearly reflects the fact that communicating learning is peripheral to a school's core purpose: learning. Communicating learning, however, is required, so the diagram shows that summative assessment scores need to be collected in a standards- (or outcomes-) based gradebook. Teachers then use their professional judgment to determine grades and to provide report cards that include comments about strengths, areas for improvement, and next steps.

Learning and the Purposes of Assessment

There are several things, in my experience, that are essential to remember about learning:

- It is the learner who does (and controls) the learning.

- Learning is frequently a messy process.

- Learning well takes time.

The first two points relate very much to the purposes of assessment. As figure 1.1 suggests, when the learning goals have been defined and the learning plan has been established, the first step in teaching for learning is to use differentiated instruction (DI) approaches and strategies. Since 1999, many books and DVDs have been produced to help teachers and principals understand and implement DI. Figure 1.1 indicates that DI approaches and strategies are part of teaching for learning, but in order to differentiate instruction, teachers must know the competency level of their students. For this, they must use diagnostic assessment (DA)—assessments that determine the strengths of their students' knowledge and understanding and the areas in which they need improvement. As Cooper (2011, p. 43) writes, "You have to have DA before you can do DI!" He continues:

> That's also my advice to teachers when I introduce the topic of differentia-
> tion during a workshop. Whether they refer to it as diagnostic assessment,
> preassessment, or initial assessment, teachers must gather data at the start
> of a year, term, or unit, or even at the start of a lesson, to determine students'
> current levels of skill and knowledge, which in turn will enable them to dif-
> ferentiate instruction appropriately. *To begin instruction before doing this
> is, I would argue, tantamount to professional malpractice.* How do we know
> where to begin teaching if we haven't first determined where students are?
> (Cooper, 2011, p. 43, emphasis mine)

[handwritten margin note: Pre assess before DI]

When we recognize that learning is a messy process and that it is acceptable, and maybe even desirable, to make (and learn from) our mistakes, then it is obvious that effective *formative* assessment—the assessment that occurs while learning is going on—is critical to the success of teaching and learning. As figure 1.1 also shows, "opportunities for practice without grading" and "quality descriptive feedback" are required. It is also essential to involve students in the formative assessment process through self- and peer assessment, reflection, and goal setting.

"Does This Count?"

"Does this count?" is not something that one hears from students in kindergarten and first grade. However, somewhere between first and seventh grade, teachers start putting a number on everything students do regardless of purpose, and every number becomes part of the grade. Teachers have done a brilliant job of training students into "Does this count?" But if we want students to focus on learning, we have to train them out of it. Principals have an important role to play in helping teachers be clear about the purpose of each type of assessment and the appropriate use of assessment results.

Great example of no grades in real life

Once, as I watched the National Football League playoffs, it struck me that while they were learning and practicing the plays that the coaches wanted to use in the games, almost certainly some of the players made mistakes, and some grasped the plays quicker than others. But they didn't receive a score for their practice performance, and each game started with a 0–0 score. What *counted*, and is a matter of public record, is how they performed in the game. To use another example, I am a golfer and occasionally take a lesson from a golf professional. At the end of a lesson, the golf pro never says you got a B or 7 out of 10 on this lesson. What he does is give feedback and guidance that help me improve my game.

Both of these examples illustrate the ideas presented by McTighe (1997):

> The ongoing interplay between assessment and instruction, so common in the arts and athletics, is also evident in classrooms using practices such as non-graded quizzes and practice tests, the writing process, formative performance tasks, review of drafts and peer response groups. The teachers in such classrooms recognize that ongoing assessments provide feedback that enhances instruction and guides student revision. (p. 11)

In practical terms, what this means is that students ideally receive descriptive feedback without scores on all or most formative assessments. No student ever learned anything of real value by getting back a quiz that has 7/10 on it, but if the feedback identifies what the student did well and what needs improvement, then he or she is guided toward appropriate further learning. In the same way, knowing that the average score for the whole class on a quiz was 6.8/10 provides little information of value to a teacher, but if the teacher determines that many students were strong in their understanding of addition and subtraction but weak in multiplication and division, then he or she can give focused reteaching to the students who are having difficulties.

Having no or few scores on formative assessments does not mean that teachers do not keep track of how well students are doing. Teachers—and students—should track formative assessments using symbol systems (+, –, √, ×) that simply acknowledge *done* or *not done*, and sometimes acknowledge *done well*, *done OK*, or *done poorly*. Teachers need this information because, if a student is not doing the formative assessments but is achieving well, there is no issue, but if a student is not doing the formative assessments and is not achieving well, the teacher has important information to discuss with that student and the student's parents.

It is also important to recognize that older elementary students who may have experienced several years of receiving points for everything they do may be resistant to not receiving scores on their formative assessments. When this happens, principals must support teachers in persistently rejecting requests for scores.

Homework

A difficult issue, especially for parents, and one that relates to the purposes of assessment and the determination of grades, is homework. Traditionally, homework has had a very significant role in grading; I am sure that most principals reading this book can think of students who "failed" not because they didn't know or understand the learning goals but because they did little or no homework. This must be seen as an unacceptable situation. As is so often the case, the role of homework in grades depends on purpose—the purpose of the homework. Homework can be classified in four ways—as preparation, practice, extension, or integration.

If homework is *preparation*—"Do this to be ready for tomorrow (or next week or next month)"— then from an assessment point of view, it is diagnostic; the results are for the teacher to use in planning instruction and have no place in grades. We cannot hold students responsible for what happens before instruction.

Most homework, however, is part of learning and is *practice*; any such assessment of student achievement is therefore formative and, for the reasons already stated, has little place in grades. Remember: formative assessments should yield feedback, not scores. There is an additional reason why practice should not be part of grades—if a teacher gives students practice homework, the students will tend to divide into three groups:

1. Students who do not need to do the homework and for whom it is just busywork

2. Students who are not at a point in their learning where they can do the homework independently

3. Students—hopefully most of them—who can benefit from the practice because it will deepen their understanding

We cannot hold the first two groups responsible for doing the homework, and if we say to the third group, "This is going to be scored, and the score will be part of your grades," the message to these students is that it is all about compliance, not learning. If it is about compliance, all that matters is that it be done, and it doesn't matter who does it—the student, a parent or guardian, a sibling, or a friend. If, on the other hand, it is about learning, it makes no sense for anyone *other* than the learner to do it. So if we want practice homework to be about learning, it is essential that it not be part of grades.

The decisions that need to be made about homework are very clearly set out in the Homework Decision Tree (figure. 1.2, page 18) developed by one of the Boards of Cooperative Educational Services (BOCES) in New York State. It highlights two aspects of homework that we need to be clear about—its purpose and who does it.

The procedure of not including formative assessments or homework in grades sometimes receives a negative response from teachers and parents; the reasoning is that if it doesn't count, students won't do it. However, we need to have the same understanding about homework we have with regard to band or basketball; practice counts. The message students should get is that everything counts—some things as practice, some as performance—and that, usually, the better the practice, the better the performance.

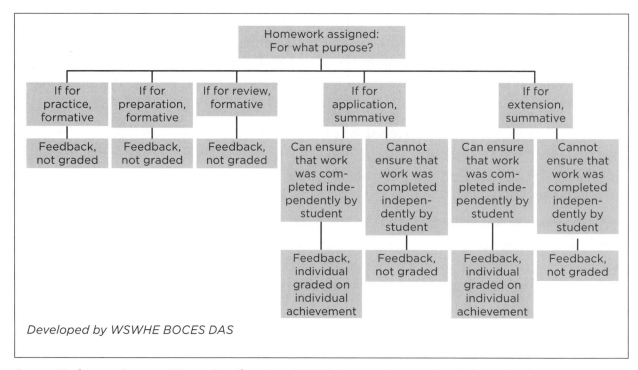

Developed by WSWHE BOCES DAS

Source: Washington Saratoga Warren Hamilton Essex BOCES, Saratoga Springs, New York. Used with permission.

Figure 1.2: The homework decision tree.

The ideas presented in this section are clearly shown in figure 1.3 (page 19). Diagnostic and practice events are tracked by the teacher or student, but only the achievement items are recorded and used for grading purposes. Note also that a distinction is made between the skills of independence and cooperation that should be tracked and reported and academic achievement items that are for recording and grading. This distinction will be the focus of chapter 2.

Using the Homework Decision Tree (figure 1.2) or the process identified in figure 1.3, principals should be able to get teachers—both new and veteran—to understand the role of homework in learning and grading.

You may have noticed that I said grades should come "primarily" from summative assessment. When teachers have moved away from the traditional practice of including everything in students' grades and have developed a deep understanding of using assessment for learning, and when it is time to make a professional judgment about the level of student achievement, I believe teachers should consider everything they know about a student. Note, however, that this is not about tracking formative assessment scores, and it is not about merely number crunching to calculate a student's grade. It is about using all the evidence as part of a *holistic* judgment that maximizes the accuracy of grades.

High-Quality Feedback

The key to the effective use of formative assessment is the quality of the feedback that students receive, so it is essential that principals assist their teachers in the understanding and delivery of high-quality feedback. To explain what high-quality feedback is, let's start with what it is not:

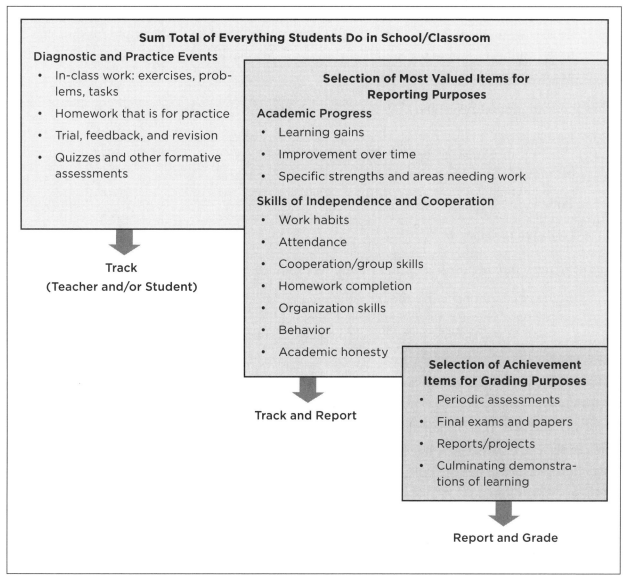

Sum Total of Everything Students Do in School/Classroom

Diagnostic and Practice Events

- In-class work: exercises, problems, tasks
- Homework that is for practice
- Trial, feedback, and revision
- Quizzes and other formative assessments

Track
(Teacher and/or Student)

Selection of Most Valued Items for Reporting Purposes

Academic Progress

- Learning gains
- Improvement over time
- Specific strengths and areas needing work

Skills of Independence and Cooperation

- Work habits
- Attendance
- Cooperation/group skills
- Homework completion
- Organization skills
- Behavior
- Academic honesty

Track and Report

Selection of Achievement Items for Grading Purposes

- Periodic assessments
- Final exams and papers
- Reports/projects
- Culminating demonstrations of learning

Report and Grade

Source: Chappuis, Jan; Stiggins, Rick; Chappuis, Steve; Arter, Judith A., Classroom Assessment for Student Learning: Doing It Right—Using It Well, *2nd edition, ©2012. Reprinted by permission of Pearson Education, Upper Saddle River, N.J. Based on the original from the work of K. O'Connor and Damian Cooper.*

Figure 1.3: Deciding what to keep track of, what to report, and how to report it.

- High-quality feedback is *not* evaluative (7 out of 10, for example) or just a rubric score (a 3 on a 4-point scale).

- High-quality feedback is *not* praise; the words *good job* or *great effort* do not tell students how to get better, although the latter is better than the former, especially if it is specific, not general. This does not mean that teachers should never use praise; Carol Dweck (2006), one of the most respected researchers in this area, "stresses the importance of using praise to encourage risk-taking and learning from failure in the classroom" as these are "experiences that make way for invention, creativity and resilience" (Chandler, 2012).

- High-quality feedback is *not* just guidance—telling students what to do to get better may help in the moment, but students need to engage with feedback, not simply do what they are told. Guidance is more useful if it is given after feedback, but teachers (and parents) often give guidance and then feedback.

So what is high-quality feedback? It is:

- Descriptive

- Specific

- Timely

- Useful to the learner

Summarizing a number of studies, Jan Chappuis (2005) writes:

> The quality of the feedback, rather than its quantity, determines its effectiveness (Bangert-Downs, Kulik, Kulik, & Morgan, 1991; Sadler, 1989). The most effective feedback identifies success and also offers students a recipe for corrective action (Bloom, 1984; Brown, 1994). Grades and other coded marks—such as + and 92%—do not tell students what areas they need to improve. Instead, such marks signal that the work on this piece is finished. (p. 41)

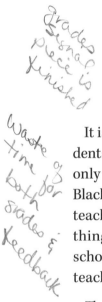

It is also essential that principals help their teachers understand it is a waste of time to give students both scores *and* descriptive feedback, because "research shows that students generally look only at grades and take little notice of the comments if provided" (Butler, 1987, as cited in Atkin, Black, & Coffey, 2001, p. 39). I wish I had known this when I was in the classroom, because I believed teachers should do both, and as a result I wasted a lot of my valuable time when I could have done things that were more effective (professionally) and more enjoyable (personally). Establishing a schoolwide procedure that formative assessment means *no mark—comment only* will truly help teachers to work smarter, not harder.

The September 2012 issue of *Educational Leadership* is devoted to "Feedback for Learning" and has articles by many of the thought leaders about formative assessment and feedback (Wiggins, Hattie, Brookhart, Wiliam, Chappuis, and Fisher and Frey). It is an excellent resource for principals and teachers.

Student Involvement

As noted earlier in this chapter, it is the learner who does (and controls) the learning, so "the better students are able to manage their learning, the better they learn" (Wiliam, 2011, p. 158). "To tip the scales in the right direction," Dylan Wiliam (2011) says that teachers should do the following:

1. Share learning goals with students so that they are able to monitor their own progress toward them.

2. Promote the belief that ability is incremental rather than fixed; when students think they can't get smarter, they are likely to devote their energy to avoiding failure.

3. Make it more difficult for students to compare themselves to others in terms of achievement.

4. Provide feedback that contains a recipe for future action rather than a view of past failures . . .

5. Use every opportunity to transfer executive control of the learning from the teacher to the students to support their development as autonomous learners. (p. 152)

Wiliam (2011) further notes that to do all of these is extremely difficult, but teachers can learn from others who have developed strategies that work. One person who has done this is Chappuis (2005, 2009; Chappuis, et al., 2012). She suggests three things that students have to know:

1. Where am I going?

2. Where am I now?

3. How can I close the gap?

Through study of research on formative assessment and motivation, Chappuis (2009) and her colleagues at the Assessment Training Institute in Portland, Oregon, have identified the following seven strategies to help students manage their own learning:

Strategy 1—Providing students with a clear understanding of the learning goal

Strategy 2—Using examples of anonymous work for students to identify strengths and weaknesses

Strategy 3—Providing frequent descriptive feedback

Strategy 4—Helping students self-assess and set goals

Strategy 5—Presenting lessons that are focused on a single learning goal or quality attribute

Strategy 6—Instructing students in focused revision

Strategy 7—Providing opportunities for students to reflect on and keep track of their learning

Strategies 1 and 2 help students know where they are going, strategies 3 and 4 help students know where they are now, and strategies 5, 6, and 7 help students close the gap. (Details on how to implement these strategies can be found in Chappuis et al., 2012; greater detail can be found in Chappuis, 2009.)

It is essential that principals make it clear that they expect their teachers to use strategies like these to develop their students as reflective learners who are able to self-assess and set goals for themselves. A powerful way to provide further opportunities for students to develop these abilities is to replace at least one set of traditional parent/teacher interviews with student-involved or student-led conferences. Please also be clear that these strategies and student-led conferencing are not just for upper elementary and middle school students; I have seen students in first grade doing wonderful self-assessment and leading excellent student conferences with their parents and teacher. Principals can find helpful information about student-involved and student-led conferences in the work of Jane Bailey and Thomas R. Guskey as well as Janet Miller-Grant, Barbara Heffler, and Kadri Mereweather.

Learning Over Time

When I was a curriculum coordinator, one of my responsibilities was elementary social studies. I needed to get to know what was happening in elementary classrooms, so in my first year in the position I spent at least half a day per week in elementary schools visiting classrooms and talking with teachers. One day in late spring, a first-grade classroom teacher asked me if I would like to see the writing samples she was going to attach to her students' end-of-year report cards. Most days, the students had written in a daily journal, but on the school day closest to the 26th of each month, they had written in a monthly journal. The teacher had photocopied the September and May journal entries for each student to attach to his or her report card and invited me to look through them.

It was fascinating to see the changes in the student's writing—both the content and the handwriting. After looking through the work of the twenty-two students, it hit me—to determine a grade for writing for these students, the September sample was irrelevant; the only sample that told me about their achievement level was the May sample. (The September sample was, however, relevant for identifying and communicating about growth.) The teaching/learning process had worked the way it is supposed to. These students had been taught and had learned—they had gone from not writing very well to doing excellent writing for first grade. So when learning is cumulative and developmental—as most learning is at the elementary level—it makes no sense to add up all the scores and calculate the average. When learning is cumulative and developmental, we must emphasize the more recent evidence, because when we have solid evidence that a student is currently achieving at a higher level, it makes the previous evidence irrelevant, and the new evidence must *replace* the old evidence. This means that grading is not just a numerical, mechanical exercise—recording scores and calculating the average—but an exercise in professional judgment. Teachers must look at the pattern of each student's performance and determine, not merely calculate, the grade.

One implication of this is that students must have multiple opportunities to demonstrate their learning. Sometimes this will happen, as in the example we just saw, with the teaching/learning plan providing the students with many opportunities to write. Sometimes, however, students will need to have the opportunity for reassessment; every teacher's objective is—or should be—proficiency for all students, so if an assessment reveals that a student is not proficient, reteaching, relearning, and reassessment are essential. Note the steps involved here—reteaching and relearning *before* reassessment; in other words, the student is, and must, be involved in "correctives" before being reassessed. It is a waste of everyone's time for students to have a reassessment if they haven't done something that increases their likelihood of success. The requirement for correctives should be an absolute condition before reassessment.

An optional condition for reassessment is the "opportunity cost"; we want students to do their best the first time, so at least some of the time, there should be a cost attached to a student having the opportunity for reassessment. That cost could be that the reassessment doesn't always take place at a time that is convenient to the student. The first reassessment opportunity may happen in class time, but subsequent reassessment opportunities may be before school, at lunchtime, or after school. An excellent way to formalize this process is shown in the form used by the World Language teachers in the Howard-Suamico School District in Green Bay, Wisconsin (figure 1.4). Students can retake assessments for full credit, but they must reflect on why they need the retake and indicate what they will do to prepare for it. The date and time are assigned by the teacher, and the student, parent, and teacher all sign the form.

[handwritten margin note: To add an "opportunity cost" (punishment) set app for reassessment outside of class]

Assessment Retake Reflection
Assessments may be retaken for full credit.

Directions:
1. Student fills in retake reflection and brings to teacher.
2. Teacher adds to steps to prepare, fills in retake date, and signs.
3. Student signs form.
4. Student takes form home to share with parent/guardian for signature.
5. Student/teacher staples original assessment to this form and brings it to the retake.

Assessment to be retaken: _____

Date the retake must be completed by (teacher fills in): _____
(Retake must be completed within two weeks of the assessment being returned to the student.)

Grade on first assessment: _____ Goal for retake: _____

Reason for needing to retake the assessment (be specific):
_____
_____

Steps I will take to prepare for the retake (be specific; teacher may add items as well):
_____
_____

Date and time I am coming in for retake (teacher fills in): _____
(Arrangements must be made with teacher.)

Teacher signature: _____
Student name: _____ Student signature: _____
Parent signature: _____

Source: Bay View Middle School, Howard-Suamico School District, Green Bay, Wisconsin. Used with permission.

Figure 1.4: Assessment retake reflection.

I would like to use another personal example to illustrate this further. Many, many years ago in a country far away, I failed the driving test for my driver's license, because my parallel parking did not meet the required standard. I immediately booked an appointment for a week later to retake the test. I am pleased to tell you that I passed on my second attempt, but there were "correctives" and "opportunity costs" involved. The correctives were practicing parking every day, and the opportunity costs were the time I put into practicing, the time I put into taking the second test, and the fee I had to pay to take it. I would have far rather passed the first time, but the availability of a second chance enabled me to get my driver's license, and in fifty years of driving, I have parked successfully thousands of times and have had only two minor accidents. It is also important to note that when I received my driver's license, it did not have stamped on it "Passed at the Second Attempt." My driver's license looked exactly like that of someone who passed on the first or fifth attempt, because the issue wasn't *when* I demonstrated the necessary competency; the issue was *whether* I demonstrated competency. That is the situation in standards-based classrooms, and that is why it is essential that principals support teachers in determining grades by emphasizing the more recent evidence.

Summary

This chapter emphasizes the principle that school is about learning, not the accumulation of points. It sets out how, in the assessment and grading process, we can honor and emphasize learning. We do this by acknowledging that learning is a messy process that takes time and that students need risk-free opportunities to see how their learning is going. This means we have to be clear about the purpose of assessment and not use evidence from formative assessments in the determination of grades. We must also use strategies that involve students in the assessment process and help them become good at self-assessment and goal setting. And it means that when learning is cumulative and developmental, we cannot just add up the scores and calculate the average—students must have multiple opportunities to show what they know, understand, and can do, and the more recent evidence should determine their grade.

2

Grading That's Accurate

The second critical attribute of grades is accuracy. Principals must ensure that the grades students receive are *accurate* because very important decisions are made about and by students on the basis of those grades. If the decisions are based on inaccurate grades, then obviously they will not be good decisions. To be accurate, grades must measure student achievement as precisely as possible. This means that skills of independence and cooperation must be tracked and reported separately from achievement. This is done by utilizing what I call "expanded-format reporting"— report cards that have a separate section for reporting student behaviors.

The story that follows provides an example of common practice that results in inaccurate grades and clearly illustrates the need for expanded-format reporting:

> When Vicki Madden of New York City saw her son Sam's fifth-grade report card, she was dismayed—and more than a little confused. Last year Sam had received 3's and 4's (on a scale of 1 to 4) in social studies, which was one of his favorite classes. But this time, despite getting 3's in the subcategories for knowledge and analytic skills, Sam's overall grade was a 1. "I asked myself how he could master the material and still fail," says Vicki, 51, a social studies teacher at a school for 6th- to 12th-graders. "It didn't make sense."
>
> After talking with Sam, who was equally perplexed, Vicki arranged a meeting with his teacher, who explained that he was doing fine on tests, but performing poorly when it came to completing take-home assignments. "She made it clear she was grading him for his work habits—not on what he knew about the subject," says Vicki. She and husband Jim, 48, a painter, started planning how to help Sam turn things around. A weekly homework checklist—what was assigned, what was completed and when—was e-mailed back and forth between the Maddens and Sam's teacher. Vicki and Jim agreed to monitor their son more closely, and question him if something was turned in late or incomplete—or not at all.
>
> Their efforts paid off: On his next report card, Sam's overall social studies grade was a 3. "It was a huge relief," says Vicki. Still, she wishes that his school's grading system was different. "Teachers have so many students and so little time to communicate. It would be better if report cards were more direct and clear about kids' academic progress," she says. "The way it is now

is a mystery, and it took digging and valuable time for us to identify Sam's problem and fix it." (Tyre, 2012)

The situation Vicki found herself in happens frequently around North America, because teachers include a variety of factors in grades. This has been called "hodgepodge grading," because so many diverse factors are included in the determination of grades that it is impossible to determine what the grade means. In traditional grading, some students get an A because they achieved at a high level and behaved well, while other students get an A despite achievement that is at the level of a B- or even a C, because they attend class every day with the correct equipment, eagerly participate in classroom activities, do extra-credit assignments, are enthusiastic and helpful, and always hand back early their permission slips and report cards signed by their parents. There are also students who get Cs and Ds because their achievement and behavior are mediocre, while other students who get Cs and Ds achieve at a very high level but do not exhibit the positive behaviors just described. The worst (or best) example of this that I have heard of is a seventh-grade student in Alberta who received a failing grade for mathematics on his school final report card but a score of 97 percent on the provincial mathematics test. He was probably a student with behavioral issues, but his mathematics achievement was not reflected in his grade. Both his high academic achievement and his behavior would have been communicated accurately if his school had used expanded-format reporting instead of hodgepodge grading.

Expanded-Format Reporting

An example of expanded reporting can be found in Lawrence, Kansas, where schools report from kindergarten through third grade on the following fifteen "Successful Learner Behaviors" (see appendix C for a complete third-grade report card):

1. Shows acceptance of others and ideas

2. Respects others (teachers, substitutes, para-educators, student teachers, peers, and so on)

3. Actively listens

4. Responds appropriately to feedback

5. Uses materials purposely and respectfully

6. Follows directions

7. Uses organizational strategies; organizes classroom materials/personal belongings

8. Uses time effectively and constructively

9. Strives to produce quality work

10. Completes tasks on time (classwork/homework)

11. Manages transitions and changes in routines

12. Exercises self-control

13. Accepts responsibility for behavior

14. Works quietly and stays on task

15. Uses cooperation skills (whole group, small group, partners)

This is a very comprehensive list and probably represents the largest number of behaviors that should be included. A smaller number—maybe a maximum of seven or eight—would be sufficient. This, of course, does not mean that these are the only behaviors that are valued—a school or school district should decide what behaviors it values, prioritize them, and then decide how many they want to include on the report card.

A set of learner behaviors that is worthy of consideration as the base for expanded-format reporting can be found in the work of the Partnership for 21st Century Skills (2011). The organization's *Framework for 21st Century Learning* identifies core subjects, 21st century themes, and 21st century interdisciplinary themes, as well as the following skills that could be stated on an expanded-format report card:

- Learning and Innovation Skills

  › Creativity and innovation

  › Critical thinking and problem solving

  › Communication and collaboration

- Information, Media, and Technology Skills

  › Information literacy

  › Media literacy

  › ICT (information, communications, and technology) literacy

- Life and Career Skills

  › Flexibility and adaptability

  › Initiative and self-direction

  › Social and cross-cultural skills

  › Productivity and accountability

  › Leadership and responsibility

A detailed description of these skills can be found at the Partnership for 21st Century Skills (2009) website (www.p21.org).

Another excellent framework principals should consider is Costa's *Habits of Mind* (Costa & Kallick, 2000). Costa identified the following sixteen dispositions as valuable in the pursuit of learning (Habits of Mind, n.d.):

1. Persisting
2. Managing impulsivity
3. Listening with empathy and understanding
4. Thinking flexibly
5. Metacognition
6. Striving for accuracy
7. Questioning and posing problems
8. Applying past knowledge to new situations
9. Creating, imagining and innovating
10. Finding humor
11. Gathering data through all senses
12. Remaining open to continuous learning
13. Responding with wonderment and awe
14. Taking responsible risks
15. Thinking and communicating with clarity and precision
16. Thinking interdependently

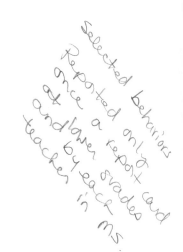

Sixteen is probably too large a number to report on at one time, but the dispositions can be divided so that a smaller number are selected on a rotating basis for each report card. One middle school that I visited focused its teaching and reported on four habits of mind each quarter. This meant that each habit of mind was reported on three times for each student as he or she moved through middle school.

After deciding which behaviors and skills to include, a decision has to be made about whether they will be reported once for each student or whether each teacher will report separately on the behaviors. This usually depends on how much time each student spends with a teacher. In the Lawrence Public Schools, from kindergarten to fifth grade, years during which a student usually spends most of the day with one teacher, the behaviors are reported only once (see appendix C), but for sixth through eighth grade, where students are taught by different teachers for each subject, at least some of the behaviors are reported separately by each teacher. Thus, in sixth grade (see appendix D), eight behaviors are reported by each teacher for each student as follows:

1. Responds appropriately to others' ideas and feedback

2. Uses cooperation and communication skills

3. Exercises self-control

4. Uses materials purposely and respectfully

5. Uses organizational strategies

6. Actively listens, follows directions

7. Stays on task, completes tasks on time

8. Strives to produce quality work

If there is any doubt about whether the behaviors should be reported together or separately by each teacher, I suggest that, for two reasons, each teacher should report them separately. The first is that combining different teachers' evaluations often makes the summary judgment meaningless, and the second is that it is time-consuming for teachers to share the evaluations and decide on the combined rating.

Other Causes of Inaccurate Grades

Accurate grading also requires that grades not be distorted by *penalties* (for late homework or academic dishonesty, for example); that *extra credit* and *attendance*—or the lack of it—not be factored directly into grades; that grades be based *on individual, not group, scores*; and that grades arise from scores on *high-quality assessments*. Some of these factors are not significant in the early elementary years, but all of them occur at one or more grade levels in many elementary schools.

Penalties

Teachers have often used mark penalties to punish students for inappropriate behaviors. I believe there are three reasons why teachers should never do this. First, these penalties distort student achievement, making the grade an inaccurate record. Second, the penalties don't work, because they don't lead to a change in behavior. My experience, and the experience of many other teachers I have spoken with, shows that the same student who turns in work late during week three and is penalized often hands work in late during weeks six and nine. Third, the penalties negatively impact motivation, especially if they are severe; students know they cannot recover from the penalty, and they are likely to continue with the inappropriate behavior.

Penalties distort grades and don't work

Late Work

Students who hand in work (that is, required assessment evidence) late clearly have one or more problems. They may be organizationally challenged, or there may be issues in their life outside of school that make it difficult to complete work outside the classroom. There are four components to effectively dealing with this problem:

1. Support—not punishment

2. Behavior and learning skill

3. Clarity and communication

4. Consequences

First, teachers must support, not punish, these students; instead of penalizing them, they must find out why they are submitting work late and work with them to overcome their difficulties. Second, they must see handing work in late as a behavior or learning issue and keep any evaluation of this behavior separate from evaluation of achievement. Third, there must be clarity in the requirements for assignments and clear communication with students and parents about timelines and how students are or are not meeting those timelines. This communication should be ongoing, as needed, and should be summarized in the appropriate place on an expanded report card. Fourth, rather than penalties, there should be appropriate consequences. Appropriate consequences are those that lead to the work being done, and they are appropriate because, if it is important assessment evidence, it is better that it be done late than not at all. These consequences generally require students who have not submitted work in a timely manner to attend sessions before school, at lunchtime, after school, or in a support period in the daily or weekly schedule during which they will receive the help and support they need to get the work done. (An example of this type of approach can be found in O'Connor, 2009, p. 102.)

 ## Academic Dishonesty

Cheating and plagiarism are unacceptable behaviors, but they *are* behaviors and need to be dealt with as such. All schools and districts have discipline codes to deal with unacceptable behaviors, and this is where the basic consequences for academic dishonesty should be found. The assessment consequence should be "do it again, *honestly,*" because, to evaluate the student's achievement, the teacher needs untainted evidence of what the student knows, understands, or can do. I believe that the double consequence—behavioral discipline and repeating the assessment—sends a clear message that academic dishonesty is unacceptable.

I have set out what I believe should be the consequences for academic dishonesty, but especially at the elementary level, our approach to academic dishonesty must be educative, not punitive. Time and effort must be put into helping students understand what are acceptable and unacceptable behaviors, and when unacceptable behavior is detected, there must be communication with parents and attempts to identify why the student is behaving inappropriately.

 ## Extra Credit

Teachers sometimes provide students with opportunities to obtain "extra credit" to boost their grades. However, if these opportunities do not involve demonstration of achievement, they inflate and result in inaccurate grades. Examples that I have heard include extra credit for bringing in food for the food drive, bringing in classroom supplies like tissues, not using bathroom passes, returning signed report cards and permission forms, and attending school events. This type of extra credit should be unacceptable and should be prohibited by school or district policy or procedures.

Another type of extra credit is provided by bonus questions on tests. For example, a test may have questions worth 50 points, but there are four bonus questions worth an additional 20 points; the teacher bases scores on 50, but the base was really 70. There are two problems with this; the first is the arithmetic distortion; the more serious problem is that the bonus questions are almost always the questions that deal with concepts and require higher-order thinking. The answers to these questions enable teachers to tell the difference between students who are excelling and those who are proficient. This is critical for teachers, so the bonus questions shouldn't be optional ("Do them if you feel like it"); all students should attempt them, so that teachers can see the full range of performance for each student. (Examples of school policies dealing with extra credit can be found in O'Connor, 2011, p. 36–37.)

Attendance

Standards-based education is about what and how well students know, understand, and do. It is not about seat time, so there is no place for school or district procedures that allow attendance or absence to directly impact the determination of grades. Students need to attend regularly to learn—it is of course also a legal requirement—but if they do not attend, methods other than reducing grades must be used to get them to school. For report card purposes, all that needs to be done is to list the number of days present or absent somewhere on the card.

It is also important to emphasize that while it may be necessary to distinguish between excused and unexcused absences for funding and legal reasons, it is inappropriate to distinguish between them for assessment and grading purposes. For those purposes, all we need to know is, was the student present, and did he or she provide evidence of learning?

Individual, Not Group Scores

Cooperative learning is one of the most powerful teaching and learning strategies that teachers have to help students achieve at high levels, but as the name implies, it is a learning, not an assessment, strategy. Unfortunately, when students engage in cooperative learning, teachers often give the same score to all the students in a group for the product that resulted from the activity. It is essential that principals see this as unacceptable. Since there is only one student's name on each report card, the evidence used to determine that student's grades should be evidence of the achievement of that student only and shouldn't be distorted by the achievement or behavior of others.

No less an authority than Spencer Kagan (1995) states that "by eliminating group grades, we will not only make grading fairer and more meaningful, but also remove a major source of resistance to cooperative learning" (p. 71). While the cooperative learning is occurring, the teacher should individually assess each student's group skills, and after the cooperative learning activities are completed, there must be individual assessment to find out what each student knows, understands, and can do as a result of the cooperative learning.

High-Quality Assessments

For grades to have any possibility of being accurate, the assessments used to gather evidence about student achievement must be high quality. Many books and journal articles have been published since the 1990s to help principals and teachers understand the differences between sound and unsound classroom assessment practices. Rick Stiggins was a pioneer and has been a leader in focusing on quality classroom assessment. To summarize the essential elements of quality assessment, I will use the model developed by Stiggins and his colleagues at the Assessment Training Institute in Portland, Oregon (figure 2.1).

Key 1: Clear Purpose
Who will use the information?
How will they use it?
What information, in what detail, is required?

Key 2: Clear Targets
Are learning targets clear to teachers?
What kinds of achievement are to be assessed?
Are these learning targets the focus of instruction?

Key 3: Sound Design
Do assessment methods match learning targets?
Does the sample represent learning appropriately?
Are items, tasks, and scoring rubrics of high quality?
Does the assessment control for bias?

Key 4: Effective Communication
Can assessment results be used to guide instruction?
Do formative assessments function as effective feedback?
Is achievement tracked by learning target and reported by standard?
Do grades communicate achievement accurately?

Key 5: Student Involvement
Do assessment practices meet students' information needs?
Are learning targets clear to students?
Will the assessment yield information that students can use to self-assess and set goals?
Are students tracking and communicating their evolving learning?

Source: Chappuis, Jan; Stiggins, Rick; Chappuis, Steve; Arter, Judith A., Classroom Assessment for Student Learning: Doing It Right—Using It Well, *2nd edition, ©2012. Reprinted by permission of Pearson Education, Upper Saddle River, N.J.*

Figure 2.1: Keys to quality classroom assessment.

Keys 1, 2, 4, and 5 are addressed in other parts of this book, so here I will focus on the components of Key 3: Sound Design.

Do Assessment Methods Match Learning Targets?

To get accurate evidence from assessments, teachers must use the method that matches the learning target. (An excellent chart providing detailed information about target-method matching can be found in Chappuis et al., 2012, p. 94.) When teachers are assessing recall knowledge, selected response is an effective and efficient option, but if they are assessing skills, then they must use performance assessment to find out how proficient the student is in using and applying the skill. For example, we do not know how well students write by asking multiple-choice questions about how to write; we find this out by having students perform writing tasks. Principals should occasionally collect their teachers' assessments and analyze whether there is a target-method match.

Does the Sample Represent Learning Appropriately?

Assessment is a sampling procedure—we cannot assess everything, so we have to collect enough evidence to be able to make accurate judgments about student achievement. Measurement experts suggest that to make a judgment about anything, we need at least three pieces of evidence; this is because the first may be luck, chance, or measurement error in one direction; the second may be luck, chance, or measurement error in the other direction; and the third will usually confirm the first or the second piece of evidence. Ideally, we probably should have a little more than three pieces of evidence, maybe four or five, but we do not need fifteen or twenty-five. Teachers have tended to over- rather than under-sample, so principals can help teachers work smarter by examining their assessment plans and gradebooks and providing guidance with regard to appropriate sampling.

Another aspect of sampling that is very important is variety in assessment methods. For most learning targets, students should be provided with opportunities to show that they understand, know, and can do, not just on selected-response and short-answer paper-and-pencil tests, but also (age-appropriately) through extended written response, performance assessment, and personal communication (interviews, oral tests, and so on). Observation and conversation are legitimate ways to collect evidence, and if you want your teachers to have accurate evidence of student achievement, you must check to see that their assessment plans include opportunities for students to "write, do and say" (Cooper, 2011, p. 114).

Are Items, Tasks, and Scoring Rubrics of High Quality?

To a large extent, quality in items, tasks, and rubrics means that each of these is well written. Directions, prompts, and rubrics need to be written in language that is clear and unambiguous, and at a reading level that is appropriate for the students being assessed. If a fifth-grade science test is written at a seventh-grade reading level, it is a reading test, not a science test, and will not provide evidence about what students know about science. Principals can help teachers ensure that their assessments are well written by providing time and encouraging teachers to share and discuss the assessments they are using in their individual classrooms.

Does the Assessment Control for Bias?

In any assessment situation there can be bias in three areas—student issues, setting, and the assessment itself—that results in the collection of inaccurate evidence of student achievement.

Student issues may include test anxiety, poor health, and lack of either testwiseness or reading skill. Dealing with these is primarily the responsibility of the classroom teacher. If any of these problems is identified, the teacher should provide support and accommodations for the student.

Setting issues include room temperature, noise, and the comfort of chairs and desks. These are usually well controlled, but if problems arise, teachers must make appropriate adjustments to ensure that students are not negatively affected.

Issues with the assessment itself are mostly those described in the characteristics of sound design already mentioned, but there is one additional problem that often distorts student achievement—insufficient time. If speed is a condition of proficiency, it is appropriate for an assessment to occur within strict time limits, but if speed is not a condition of quality, all students should have enough time to show what they know, understand, and can do. It is appropriate for trainee air-traffic controllers to be assessed within strict time limits, but little if anything in classroom assessment resembles air-traffic control; thus, most assessments should involve flexible rather than fixed time. Students who know, understand, and can do equally well write and think at different speeds, and those who write and think slowly should not be penalized—unless speed is a condition of quality. The drawbacks of timed assessment in mathematics are expressed clearly by mathematics teaching expert Marilyn Burns (2000), who writes:

> What about using timed tests to help children learn their basic facts? This makes no instructional sense. Children who perform well under time pressure display their skills. Children who have difficulty with skills, or who work more slowly, run the risk of reinforcing wrong learning under pressure. In addition, children can become negative and fearful toward their math learning. Also, timed tests do not measure children's understanding. . . . they don't ensure that students will be able to use the facts in problem-solving situations. Furthermore, it conveys to children that memorizing is the way to mathematical power, rather than learning to think and reason to figure out answers. (p. 157)

Summary

In this chapter, I have described what is essential for principals to be aware of and monitor to ensure that grades are accurate. Accuracy requires that grades be about achievement only, with the use of expanded-format reporting to give information about the behaviors that principals, teachers, and parents value—behaviors that mistakenly are often included in grades, making it impossible to know what a grade really means with regard to achievement. Grading that is only about achievement also requires that penalties not be applied to grades for late and missing work, academic dishonesty, and absences; that extra credit be prohibited; and that grades be based on individual achievement, not group scores. Accuracy also requires that the evidence used to determine grades come from high-quality assessment.

3

Grading That's Meaningful

To ensure that grading and reporting are effective forms of communication, grades and report cards must provide a third essential characteristic—meaningful information. Typically, grades have been for subjects, and traditional report cards have provided only one letter grade for each subject, as shown in figure 3.1.

Pleasantdale School
Report Card

Teacher: Mrs. Langer   **Year:** 2012

Student: Joseph Marathi   **Grade:** 6

Subject	Grade
English	A
Mathematics	B
Social Studies	B
Science	B
French	B
Physical Education	A
Art	D
Music	B

Figure 3.1: A traditional report card.

While this kind of report provides information that has some value in giving a general impression of student achievement, it does not provide meaningful information that can be used to help students improve. To provide meaningful information, it is essential that grading and reporting be standards based and give a profile of student achievement in each subject. Instead of reporting a B for mathematics, we need to grade and report on achievement with regard to specific mathematics standards.

A sporting analogy will illustrate this. As I have mentioned, I occasionally take lessons from a golf professional. He expects me to bring him my scorecards from the last few rounds I have played before the lesson, and he expects that on those scorecards I have entered a lot more information than just my score for each hole and the round. He glances at my scores, but he focuses on the details—fairways hit, greens in regulation, number of putts, number of approach shots, and so on. He does this because my scores alone give him no meaningful information to help me improve, but by looking at the specifics, he is able to identify my current strengths and weaknesses and plan the lesson in such a way that they will help me perform better.

How to Use Standards

Fortunately, standards-based grading and reporting, as seen in appendices C and D for Lawrence, Kansas (pages 73–85), have become very common in elementary schools. If you are not using standards-based grading and reporting, or if you are reviewing your current approach, there are a number of important issues that need to be considered with regard to how the content standards are used in the grading and reporting process. These include how many standards to use, the level of specificity, whether the standards will be grade-level-specific or include several grades, whether the reports will use parent-friendly or official language, and whether there will be grades for subjects as well as standards. There also needs to be agreement on terminology. Definitions used by the CCSS* of three of the important terms involving standards follow.

Definitions of Standards Terms

Standards define specifically what a student should understand and be able to do.

Content standard **clusters** are groups of related standards.

Domains are larger groups of related standards. (Before the Common Core, these were often referred to as "strands.")

(NGA & CCSSO 2010, pp. 44–45)

How Many Standards and at What Level of Specificity?

Obviously, teachers plan instruction and teach and assess student achievement at a very specific level, but grading and reporting are communication processes in which we *summarize* information. If we reported on every specific learning goal, teachers' gradebooks would be as thick as phone books, and the report card would be the size of a book. That would be overwhelming for parents and too burdensome for teachers, so decisions have to be made about how many standards and at which level of specificity the information will be recorded. You can see in appendix C (page XX) that, at the third-grade level, Lawrence has four strands (domains) in its mathematics curriculum (Number Sense and Computation; Algebra, Patterns and Functions; Statistics, Data, and Probability; and Geometry and Measurement) and chose to report on twenty-six specific standards. Lincoln Public

---

* The Common Core State Standards Initiative seeks to bring diverse U.S. state curricula into alignment using standards-based principles. The CCSS is sponsored by the National Governors Association (NGA) and the Council of Chief State School Officers (CCSSO).

Schools in Nebraska (figure 3.2), by contrast, provides grades for six mathematics strands (domains)—Numeration and Number Sense, Computation and Estimation, Measurement, Geometry, Data Analysis and Probability, and Algebra—and what they label as mathematical processes (Problem Solving; Develops Conceptual Understanding; and Work/Study Habits). Neither approach is "right"; each has advantages and disadvantages that need to be considered. For example, a case could be made that twenty-six pieces of information is too much for teachers to record, that it is too detailed for parents, and that when combined with other subjects at a similar level of specificity, it is just too much for everyone involved. On the other hand, a case can be made that reporting only at the strand level does not provide enough detail.

Mathematics

Mathematics Content	Q1	Q2	Q3	Q4
Numeration and Number Sense • Reads, writes, and compares whole numbers through 1,000 • Reads and uses fraction word names				
Computation and Estimation • Adds and subtracts 2-digit numbers with and without regrouping • Uses standard units for length, capacity, and weight				
Measurement • Tells time to 5-minute intervals • Uses standard units for length, capacity, and weight				
Geometry • Identifies congruent figures • Identifies lines of symmetry				
Data Analysis and Probability • Finds simple probability • Interprets graphs				
Algebra • Writes addition and subtraction sentences • Solves addition and subtraction word problems				
Mathematical Processes	Q1	Q2	Q3	Q4
Problem Solving				
Develops Conceptual Understanding				
Work/Study Habits				

Source: Lincoln Public Schools, Lincoln, Nebraska. Used with permission.

Figure 3.2: Second-grade mathematics report card.

In table 3.1 Guskey and Bailey (2010, p. 38) helpfully identify the differences between curriculum standards and reporting standards.

Table 3.1: Curriculum Standards vs. Reporting Standards

Curriculum Standards	Reporting Standards
Designed for planning instruction and assessments	Designed for reporting on student learning
Many in number (10–50 per subject)	Relatively few in number (usually 4–6 per subject)
Highly specific	Broad and more general
Complicated and detailed	Clear and understandable
Expressed in complex, educator language	Expressed in parent-friendly language

Given that the Common Core State Standards have now been adopted by forty-six states and the District of Columbia, I will use the fifth-grade mathematics standards (NGA & CCSSO, 2010) to illustrate how these differences between curriculum standards and reporting standards play out in practice. There are five of what Guskey and Bailey would call reporting standards (called "domains" in the Common Core) and twenty-six curriculum standards, both falling within the range suggested by Guskey and Bailey (2010), as shown in table 3.1. The Common Core mathematics domains are:

1. Operations and Algebraic Thinking

2. Number and Operations in Base Ten

3. Number and Operations—Fractions

4. Measurement and Data

5. Geometry

They are broad and general, clear, and understandable, and are in somewhat parent-friendly language. To enable you to see some of the differences, the specific curriculum standards for the fifth-grade Number and Operations in Base Ten domain (5.NBT) are shown in figure 3.3. This domain has two content standard clusters, "Understand the place value system" with four standards and "Perform operations with multi-digit whole numbers and with decimals to hundredths" with three standards.

Number and Operations in Base Ten (NBT) Domain

Content Standard Clusters for Grade 5

Understand the place value system.

- 5.NBT.1. Recognize that in a multi-digit number, a digit in one place represents 10 times as much as it represents in the place to its right and $\frac{1}{10}$ of what it represents in the place to its left.

- 5.NBT.2. Explain patterns in the number of zeros of the product when multiplying a number by powers of 10, and explain patterns in the placement of the decimal point when a decimal is multiplied or divided by a power of 10. Use whole-number exponents to denote powers of 10.

- 5.NBT.3. Read, write, and compare decimals to thousandths.

  + Read and write decimals to thousandths using base-ten numerals, number names, and expanded form, e.g., $347.392 = 3 \times 100 + 4 \times 10 + 7 \times 1 + 3 \times (\frac{1}{10}) + 9 \times (\frac{1}{100}) + 2 \times (\frac{1}{1000})$.

  + Compare two decimals to thousandths based on meanings of the digits in each place, using >, =, and < symbols to record the results of comparisons.

- 5.NBT.4. Use place value understanding to round decimals to any place.

Perform operations with multi-digit whole numbers and with decimals to hundredths.

- 5.NBT.5. Fluently multiply multi-digit whole numbers using the standard algorithm.
- 5.NBT.6. Find whole-number quotients of whole numbers with up to four-digit dividends and two-digit divisors, using strategies based on place value, the properties of operations, and/or the relationship between multiplication and division. Illustrate and explain the calculation by using equations, rectangular arrays, and/or area models.
- 5.NBT.7. Add, subtract, multiply, and divide decimals to hundredths, using concrete models or drawings and strategies based on place value, properties of operations, and/or the relationship between addition and subtraction; relate the strategy to a written method and explain the reasoning used.

Source: National Governors Association Center for Best Practices, Washington, D.C., Council of Chief State School Officers. (2010). Common Core State Standards: Mathematics.

Figure 3.3: Mathematics grade 5 number and operations in base ten.

The curriculum standards are numerous (there are twenty-six of them), very specific, very detailed, somewhat complicated, and expressed in teacher language, so it would be inappropriate to use them all for grading and reporting. However, if greater detail than the domain level is seen as desirable, there are two alternatives. The first is to use the categorization provided within the standards, that is, the clusters, and the second would be to choose up to ten of the most important standards and express them in parent-friendly language.

Using the clusters for each domain in figure 3.3, eleven standards can be identified for reporting, as shown in table 3.2.

Table 3.2: Clusters for Each Domain of Grade 5 Mathematics Reporting Standards

Domains	Clusters Used as Reporting Standards
Operations and Algebraic Thinking (5.OA)	Write and interpret numerical expressions.
	Analyze patterns and relationships.
Number and Operations in Base Ten (5.NBT) Number and Operations—Fractions (5.NF)	Understand the place value system.
	Perform operations with multidigit whole numbers and decimals to hundredths.
	Use equivalent fractions to add and subtract fractions.
	Multiply and divide fractions.
Measurement and Data (5.MD)	Convert like measurement units.
	Represent and interpret data.
Geometry (5.G)	Understand the concept of volume.
	Graph points on the coordinate plane.
	Classify two-dimensional figures.

(handwritten margin note: example of using cluster titles as "reporting standards")

An alternative would be to select the most important standards. This could be done by choosing the two most important from each domain, or if there were a greater number of very important standards in one domain, by choosing fewer standards from the other domains. (Thanks to Sarah Craig for selecting these and to Janna Smith for reviewing this section on the grade 5 mathematics standards.) Selecting the most important, the reporting standards might be as follows:

- Write and interpret simple expressions. (5.OA.2)

- Generate two numerical patterns using two given rules. (5.OA.3)

- Read, write, and compare decimals to thousandths. (5.NBT.3)

- Perform operations with multidigit whole numbers and decimals. (5.NBT.5)

- Multiply and divide using fractions and whole numbers. (5.NF.4 and 5.NF.7)

- Make line plots and solve problems involving information presented in line plots. (5.MD.2)

- Solve real-world and mathematical problems involving volume. (5.MD.5)

- Graph points in the first quadrant of the coordinate plane, and interpret coordinate values of points in the context of the situation. (5.G.2)

- Understand that attributes belonging to a category of two-dimensional figures also belong to all subcategories of that category. (5.G.3)

- Classify two-dimensional figures. (5.G.4)

about 10 standards per subject

It is important to note that with the selection of more detailed standards there are more than the four to six for each subject recommended by Guskey and Bailey (2010). I suggest these as alternatives, because I think it is acceptable to have up to about ten standards for each subject.

To report by standards, teachers obviously have to assess and grade by standards. This means that each assessment has to be categorized by standard, and the scores students get are also for each standard. They do not receive one total score for the assessment. This is illustrated in figure 3.4 using a 4-point scale

This example is based on the use of the domains as the grading and reporting standards. Each test and performance assessment (PA) assessed standards from two or three domains, and with six assessments during the grading period, a picture emerges of each student's performance on the three domains that were the focus of instruction in this grading period.

This example suggests the use of a gradebook with one page per student. I use this example because I think it is the best way to illustrate how a gradebook needs to be organized for standards-based grading. Although I feel it is the best method for teachers to use, it requires a high degree of organizational skill and uses a lot of paper, so many principals and teachers may see it as impractical. Fortunately, there are several alternatives; probably the next best is the use of spreadsheets, because on a spreadsheet teachers can list all their students on one page and can include as many standards as they need. An example of such a spreadsheet partially filled out is shown in figure 3.5 (page 42); more examples can be found in Chappuis et al., 2012.

Common Core Grade 5 Mathematics Achievement

Student: _____

	Achievement Evidence							
	Assessments							
Domains	10/1 Test	10/15 PA	11/7 PA	11/18 PA	12/8 PA	12/17 Test	Strengths, Areas for Improvements/ Observations	Grade
Operations and Algebraic Thinking (3)	3 (17/20)	3		3	3	3 (17/20)		3
Number and Operations in Base Ten (7)					1			NA
Number and Operations— Fractions (7)	2 (15/20)		4	2	2	2 (15/20)		2
Measurement and Data (5)	4 (19/20)	4	4	1		4 (19/20)		4
Geometry (4)	3 (16/20)							NA
Comments: Numbers in ( ) in the far left column are the number of standards within each domain.								

Source: Domains are from the Common Core State Standards; chart created by Ken O'Connor; artwork developed by Heidi Bay, Grey Sky Design, Portland, Oregon

Figure 3.4: Common Core grade 5 mathematics standards–based gradebook.

Figure 3.5 shows the same data as figure 3.4 except for the data for Geometry. In this example, the scores and grades for one student for four domains are shown. There is sufficient data to determine a grade for three domains, but there is only one score for Number and Operations—Fractions, which is insufficient, so the grade is shown as NA—Not Assessed. This means that the teacher did not attempt to collect sufficient evidence. While the example provides space for recording the scores and grades for seven students, on a real spreadsheet, a teacher would enter all the students in the class.

Another alternative is the use of a computer-based grading program, like Pearson's PowerTeacher. It is set up for a standards-based approach and has considerable flexibility. Teachers can even use traditional hard-copy gradebooks and divide each page into the number of vertical columns equal to the number of reporting standards. The important point here is that, wherever teachers are on a technological continuum from hard-copy gradebook to computer-based grading programs, this type of grading can and should be done. The role of principals is to ensure that all of their teachers are doing standards-based assessment and grading and to provide them with alternatives for recording the data.

Domain	O & AT						N&O-BT		N&O-F						M&D					
Date	10/1	10/15	11/18	12/8	12/17		12/8		10/1	11/7	11/18	12/8	12/17		10/1	10/15	11/7	11/18	12/17	
Task	T	PA	PA	PA	T	Grade	PA	Grade	T	PA	PA	PA	T	Grade	T	PA	PA	PA	T	Grade
Students																				
1 S. Martinez	3	3	3	3	3	3	1	NA	2	4	2	2	2	2	4	4	4	1	4	4
2																				
3																				
4																				
5																				
6																				
7																				

Key

O&AT = Operations and Algebraic Thinking

N&O-BT = Numbers and Operations in Base Ten

N&O-F = Number and Operations (Fractions)

M&D = Measurement and Data

Figure 3.5: Sample spreadsheet showing Common Core grade 5 mathematics standards–based grades for one student.

Grade-Level Specific or the Same Standards for Several Grades?

Some schools and districts believe that it is helpful to parent understanding if the same standards are used as the base for grading and reporting in several grades. This approach is seen in the Lincoln Public Schools report card (figure 3.2, page 37). Lincoln uses the same domains for grades 1 to 5 but lists specific mathematics concepts and skills for each grade level. (For example, the grade 3 report card includes the same concepts and skills for algebra as the report card for grade 2, but the geometry concepts and skills are "Uses properties of lines and angles" and "Plots ordered pairs.") This provides standardization for general understanding and specifics for detailed discussion of student strengths and weaknesses.

Other school districts believe that the specific standards for each grade level should be in teachers' gradebooks *and* on the report card. This approach is seen in the Lawrence Public Schools report cards (appendices C and D, pages 73 and 79); the domains provide consistency, but the standards for each grade level are given.

Once again, I can't say one way is right and the other wrong. Both approaches have advantages and disadvantages, but for schools and districts in those states that have adopted the Common Core State Standards, the structure provided by those standards makes it easier. In both mathematics and English language arts, there is consistency in the domains over several grade levels, so these should be the main organizers for gradebooks and report cards, followed by some reporting standards using one of the approaches described. In English language arts, the same domains are used from grade 1 to grade 5 (Reading—Literature, Reading—Informational Texts, Reading—Foundational Skills, Writing, Speaking and Listening, Language), and these domains are also used from grade 6 to grade 12, except that Reading—Foundational Skills is omitted. Unfortunately the structure of the mathematics standards changes very significantly for grade 6 and higher. In mathematics, four domains are common to grades K–5: Operations and Algebraic Thinking, Number and Operations in Base Ten, Measurement and Data, and Geometry. The domain Counting and Cardinality applies to kindergarten only. The domain Number and Operations—Fractions applies to grades 3–5.

Parent-Friendly or State Language?

Teachers may want to use the language of the state or Common Core State Standards among themselves, but our prime consideration must be for the receiver of our communication. So when the language of the standards is not parent friendly, we need to rewrite it. The kindergarten mathematics strand Counting and Cardinality provides a prime example of this; *counting* is obviously parent friendly, but *cardinality* isn't, so an alternative word or words should be used on report cards. Principals should carefully examine the labeling of all standards on the report cards and ensure that they are in parent-friendly language.

Grades for Standards With or Without Subject Grade?

(handwritten note in left margin:) Problem with our dual report card: grades & standards

The grade 3 Lawrence Public Schools report card (appendix C) has grades only for standards, but the grade 6 report card (appendix D) requires a grade for "Overall Performance" for language arts, mathematics, science, and social science, in addition to grades for the standards. I believe those overall subject grades are inappropriate, because not only do they not add to the communication, but they frequently detract from it. They do not add to the communication, because a very rich picture of each student's performance is provided by the grades for the standards, and an overall grade does not make that picture clearer or better. Parents, students, and teachers are able to see clearly the areas of strength and the areas that need improvement. Inevitably, parents and students focus on the overall grade if it is provided and give little or no consideration to the rich picture provided by grades for standards. Furthermore, if a student performs consistently at any level, an overall grade is unnecessary, because it is obvious what the grade should be. If a student performs inconsistently, it is difficult to determine an overall grade, and the accuracy of the overall grade may become the discussion point instead of the student's strengths and areas for improvement.

For schools and districts that have taken a standards-based approach to assessment, not having subject grades is rarely an issue up to grade 3, but it is sometimes an issue after that. Some parents and teachers argue that you need subject grades in grades 4 and 5 to prepare students for middle school, and failing that, you need subject grades in grades 6 through 8 to prepare them for high school. To "prepare them for the next level" is a bad argument for at least two reasons. First, students don't need subject grades at elementary school to prepare for middle school, and they don't need grades at middle school to be prepared for high school. This is because students adapt easily to structures at each new level, especially if the schools and teachers provide clear descriptions and a rationale for whatever is being done. Second, we should do what is best for students *now*—what is best for a thirteen-year-old may not be what is best for a ten-year-old.

Principals have an essential role to play in this issue, as they must work with any resistant teachers, parents, and community members to demonstrate that there is little reason to have single-subject grades below high school. Ideally, they should be used only in grades 11 and 12—and then only because of the college admissions process.

Summary

Standards-based assessment and grading is about alignment; if your school or district is—or is supposed to be—standards based for curriculum and instruction, it should be standards based for assessment, grading, and reporting as well. This means that teachers have to plan their assessments with a standards base, their gradebooks need to be organized by standards, and report cards need to be standards based. As a principal, you may have to make decisions about the level of specificity of the standards—should they be grade-level specific or the same for several grades? Also, should they be parent friendly or use state language, and should you use grades for standards with or without a subject grade? It will also often fall to you in your role as principal to be an advocate for and a defender of standards-based grading. To that end you may find either or both of these quotes useful in discussions with teachers and parents:

The use of columns in a grade book to represent standards, instead of assignments, tests, and activities, is a major shift in thinking . . . *Under this system, when an assessment is designed, the teacher must think in terms of the standards it is intended to address.* If a [test] is given that covers three standards, then the teacher makes three entries in the grade book for each student—one entry for each standard—as opposed to one overall entry for the entire [test]. (Marzano & Kendall, 1996, p. 150; emphasis mine)

The principal limitation of any grading system that requires the teacher to assign one number or letter to represent . . . learning is that one symbol can convey only one meaning. . . . *One symbol cannot do justice to the different degrees of learning a student acquires across all learning outcomes.* (Tombari & Borich, 1999, p. 213; emphasis mine)

Resources on Standards-Based Grading

Resources that you might find useful in the support of standards-based grading and reporting are:

- Guskey, T. R., Swan, G. M., & Jung, L. A. (2011). Grades that mean something. *Phi Delta Kappan, 93*(2), 52–57.

- Marzano, R., & Kendall, J. (1996). *A comprehensive guide to developing standards-based districts, schools, and classrooms.* Aurora, CO: McREL.

- Oliver, B. (2011). Making the case for standards-based grading. *Just for the ASKing!* Available at www.justaskpublications.com/jfta/2011_1_jfta.htm.

- Quakertown Community School District. *Why standards-based grading?* Available at www .qcsd.org/213010222123447650/lib/213010222123447650/SBG_brochure.pdf.

- Tombari, M., & Borich, G. (1999). *Authentic Assessment in the Classroom.* Upper Saddle River, NJ: Merrill/Prentice Hall.

Grading That's Consistent

The last but certainly not the least important characteristic of grades is that they need to be consistent. When students and parents complain about grades to principals, it is often consistency—or the lack of it—that is at the root of the complaint: students talk to other students and parents talk to other parents, and through their talk they identify glaring inconsistencies in teachers' grading practices and in the application of district and school policies and procedures. Principals need to understand that the two essential elements that have the greatest impact on consistency in grading are the type and clarity of the performance standards that are in place and the policies and procedures that their teachers are required to implement.

Type and Clarity of Performance Standards

Performance standards are the other—and often forgotten—part of standards. Chapter 3 was basically about the "what" of learning—the content standards. Performance standards are about "how well" we expect the content standard to be performed. For there to be any possibility that grades will be consistent, every school district must have clear, well-written, public performance standards that are understood by teachers, students, and parents. The reason some teachers are considered "hard" and others "soft" is mostly because of the lack of—or the lack of clarity about—performance standards.

When performance standards are not clear, they become whatever each teacher thinks they should be. As John Kendall and Robert Marzano (1997) write, "Performance standards specify 'how good is good enough.' They relate to issues of assessment that gauge the degree to which content standards have been attained. . . . They are indices of quality that specify how adept or competent a student demonstration should be" (pp. 16–17).

Here is a simple example—a first-grade physical education standard might be "hop on one foot." How do we know a student can meet this standard? Only when we identify that the performance standard for proficiency is, say, six times on each foot. It is also important to note that we might have the same content standard for sixth grade, but proficiency might be twenty-five times on each foot.

The main problem that we have had with performance standards is that principals, teachers, schools, and districts have not put much time into the development of clear and appropriate performance standards for standards-based education. Since the introduction of state and provincial standards, huge amounts of time and effort have been put into unpacking the content standards and planning curriculum, instruction, and assessment based on those standards. This was necessary and appropriate, but for assessment and grading, the performance standards are the most important part of the standard.

One reason they have received less attention is that developing clear and useful performance standards is very difficult; in fact, the development of performance standards is probably the most difficult part of the whole process, because it requires very high-quality critical thinking and provides a challenge to our ability to use the English language clearly and precisely.

How Many Levels?

As a result of the failure to address performance standards, there has been a tendency to continue to use point- and percentage-based performance standards even though they do not "fit" a standards-based system. In a pure standards-based system, there would be only two levels (proficient and not proficient); ultimately, that is all that matters, since what we want—and need—is all-student proficiency. Ideally, we would use a two-level system throughout elementary school, but sometimes at all elementary grade levels, and almost always above first or second grade, there appears to be a desire for more than two levels. This makes some sense, because identifying a level above proficiency both acknowledges and encourages excellence, and identifying levels below proficiency acknowledges that some students are partially proficient or close to proficient while others are well below proficiency. But there is no right number of levels, so a decision has to be made, preferably within the range of two to seven levels. I suggest seven as the upper limit, because we must be able to distinguish clearly between the levels and describe them, and I do not believe that our use of language is good enough to describe more than seven.

When agreement has been reached on the number of levels, decisions have to be made on how to label, name, and describe them and on what symbols to use. The Lawrence (Kansas) Public Schools (appendices C and D, pages 78–85) use four levels, as follows (Lawrence Public Schools, n.d.):

E   **Excels**—Consistently goes beyond academic (or learner behavior) expectations.

S   **Successfully meets academic (or learner behavior) expectations**—Evidence of most recent work demonstrates that the learning goals are fully and consistently met.

M   **Making progress in meeting academic (or learner behavior) expectations**—Evidence of most recent work demonstrates that more than half the learning goals are fully and consistently met.

T   **Targeted for growth in order to meet academic (or learner behavior) expectations**—Evidence of most recent work demonstrates only a few of the learning goals are met or partially met.

It is worth noting that on the actual report cards, S is listed first, because Lawrence Public Schools believes that is the minimum level at which it wants all students to perform.

The American School of Doha (ASD) in Qatar (ASD, personal communication, November 6, 2012) also uses four levels for academic achievement but three levels for work habits and social development.* For academic achievement the levels are:

4   **Advanced**—The student consistently demonstrates an in-depth understanding of the standard/benchmark, exceeding grade-level expectations. The student applies and extends the key concepts, processes, and skills. Performance is characterized by high levels of quality and complexity.

3   **Proficient**—The student consistently demonstrates a thorough understanding of the standard/benchmark, meeting grade-level expectations. The student applies the key concepts, processes, and skills.

2   **Approaching Proficiency**—The student demonstrates some understanding of the standard/benchmark. Performance is inconsistent and varies in regard to accuracy and quality.

1   **Limited Proficiency**—The student does not demonstrate an understanding of the standard/benchmark. Student is well below grade-level expectations. Performance is inconsistent even with support.

For work habits and social development, the levels ASD uses are:

U   Usually

O   Occasionally

S   Seldom

The Lincoln Public Schools (Des Moines Public Schools, n.d.a.) also use four levels for academic achievement:

4   Exceeds district standards

3   Meets district standards

2   Approaches but does not meet district standards

1   Does not meet district standards

In addition, Lincoln uses four levels for work and study habits:

4   Exceeds expectations

---

* I should state here that I believe it is inappropriate to include words like *support* or *independence* in the descriptors for performance standards. When we are evaluating student achievement, students should always be demonstrating what they know, understand, or can do independently. This goes for students' individual education plans (IEPs); if students have an IEP, this means they will be working independently *with* the use of any modifications in their plan.

3 Meets expectations

2 Approaches expectations

1 Does not meet expectations

You can see that each of these districts or schools uses four levels, but with considerable differences in the names, labels, and descriptors. Also, Lawrence uses the same performance standards for academic achievement and work habits and behaviors, whereas ASD and Lincoln use different descriptors. For academic achievement, all three identify the second level from the top as proficient or meeting standards, but the labels and the symbols used to represent them vary. Lawrence uses symbols that come from the labels while ASD and Lincoln use numbers. Lawrence and ASD add descriptors to the labels and symbols, while Lincoln uses labels on only the report cards, with the description of the levels found in detailed rubrics for each subject. Figure 4.1 provides an example of such a rubric for second-grade English language arts.

In an article in *Kappan* magazine, Guskey (2004) provides useful advice on the development of performance standards:

1. Avoid comparative language, for example, "average."

2. Provide examples based on student work.

3. Distinguish between "Levels of Understanding" (quality) and "Frequency of Display" (quantity).

4. Be consistent (across grade levels). (pp. 327–328)

You can see that the three examples above, Lawrence, ASD, and Lincoln, have followed (possibly unknowingly) Guskey's (2004) advice with regard to points 1, 3, and 4, as they have avoided the use of comparative language; they have mostly used quality descriptors—although ASD uses quantity descriptors for behaviors; and they use these descriptors consistently across their elementary grade levels.

Mentioning consistency across grade levels requires consideration of the "elementary grade levels." For the purposes of this book, we are referring to K–8 schools regardless of the number of grade levels within each school. I agree with Guskey (2004) that it is best to be consistent across grade levels from kindergarten to grade 8, but I recognize that a strong case can be made for using only two levels at kindergarten and that frequently there is considerable pressure brought to bear to move to letter grades based on percentages at sixth, seventh, and eighth grades. However, I believe principals should take a strong stand and maintain consistency from first to eighth grade. It has become increasingly clear that the use of percentages is incompatible with standards-based education, since percentages have no meaning in and of themselves and encourage the perception that a school is concerned primarily with accumulating points and ranking students. Performance standards in a standards-based system always need to be about the *level* of performance in relation to proficiency. This means that the teacher's mark or score recording should look like those in figure 4.2 (page 52). All scores are recorded by level from the rubrics used for performance assessments (PAs).

Second Grade—Multiple Literacies				
	4 **Exceeds**	**3** **Meets**	**2** **Approaches**	**1** **Does Not Meet**
Yearlong	• Consistently selects, checks out, and returns books to media center • Consistently finds textual, visual, and digital information with some assistance, both in and out of the classroom, to answer questions • Consistently selects and reads independently materials appropriate for reading level, purpose, and interest from a variety of genres • Consistently uses drawing, writing, and conversations with others to compose opinions when listening to texts read or reading (e.g., "My favorite part . . .")	• Often selects, checks out, and returns books to media center • Often finds textual, visual, and digital information with some assistance both in and out of the classroom to answer questions • Often selects and reads independently materials appropriate for reading level, purpose, and interest from a variety of genres • Often uses drawing, writing, and conversations with others to compose opinions when listening to texts read or reading (e.g., "My favorite part . . .")	• Occasionally selects, checks out, and returns books to media center • Occasionally finds textual, visual, and digital information with some assistance both in and out of the classroom to answer questions • Occasionally selects and reads independently materials appropriate for reading level, purpose, and interest from a variety of genres • Occasionally uses drawing, writing, and conversations with others to compose opinions when listening to texts read or reading (e.g., "My favorite part . . .")	• Is unable to select, check out, and return books to media center • Is unable to find textual, visual, and digital information with some assistance both in and out of the classroom to answer questions • Is unable to select and read independently materials appropriate for reading level, purpose, and interest from a variety of genres • Is unable to use drawing, writing, and conversations with others to compose opinions when listening to texts read or reading (e.g., "My favorite part . . .")

Source: Lincoln Public Schools, Lincoln, Nebraska. Used with permission.

Figure 4.1: Lincoln Public Schools multiple literacies rubric for grade 2 English language arts.

However, for tests, which can be scored using rubrics but are most commonly scored by points, the level of performance recorded is based on the number of points received. This means that on each test, teachers must decide on the cut scores for the levels. If the concepts and skills are difficult and the questions are difficult, the cut score for the highest level should be relatively low (for example, 14/20 on fitness management is a 4 in figure 4.2, page 52), but if the concepts, skills, or questions are easy, then the cut score for the highest level should be relatively high (for example, 18/20 is required for a 4 on personal safety). Thus on every points-based test for each standard, the teacher must place a small chart indicating the cut score for each level. Everyone involved must understand that it is not appropriate to use fixed scales, for example, 90–100 = A, 80–89 = B, 70–79 = C, and so on.

Manitoba Grades 7 and 8 Physical/Health Education

Student: _____

	Achievement Evidence							
	Assessments							
Strands	10/1 PA	10/15 PA	11/7 Test	11/18 PA	12/8 PA	12/17 PA	Strengths, Areas for Improvement/ Observations	Summary
Movement	3	3	3 (16/20)	3		3		3
Fitness Management	1				NS	2		I
Physical Activity Safety					NS			NA
Personal Safety	2		4 (18/20)	2	NS	2		2
Personal/ Social Management	4	4		1		4		4
Healthy Lifestyle	1	3		4	NS	4		4

> PA = Performance assessment
>
> NS = Not submitted
>
> I = Insufficient evidence

Source: Strands/Domains are from the Manitoba Learning Outcomes; chart created by Ken O'Connor; artwork developed by Heidi Bay, Grey Sky Design, Portland, Oregon.

Figure 4.2: Manitoba grades 7 and 8 physical education standards–based gradebook.

A sports analogy may again help us understand this. In Major League Baseball, hitting .250 (an average of hitting safely 2½ times out of 10 attempts) is proficient, .300 (3/10) is excellent, and .400 (4/10) is superb and has been achieved only once in the modern era of baseball. Why is it that in baseball what would be considered a low score in other fields, especially education, represents a range from proficiency to excellence? Because hitting a baseball that is not only coming at you at over ninety miles per hour but is also moving up and down or side to side is extremely difficult. Contrast that with free throws in the National Basketball Association, where proficiency is considered to be between 70 and 80 percent, because throwing the ball into the basket with no interference by an opposing player is a lot easier than hitting a baseball. These examples illustrate clearly that performance standards are not fixed—they depend on the difficulty of the concepts or skills and, in school, on the difficulty of the assessments, and that is controlled by the teachers.

Regardless of how many levels are chosen, and whether the levels are labeled with words or symbols or both, it is essential that the words used to describe the levels be as clear as possible for all stakeholders. What is most important is that teachers are able to use them to make consistent judgments of student achievement, but it is also important that they be written in language that is understandable by parents and students. To achieve the latter, it may be necessary to have one set of descriptors for teachers and a modified set of descriptors for students or parents.

To What Period Do the Standards Apply?

Another aspect of performance standards about which clarity is needed is determining when the standards apply—when you say a student is "proficient" or "meeting standards," do you mean meeting your requirements at the time of the report card, or are you referring to what is expected at the end of the year? Whatever you decide must be clear to all. I have seen schools and districts where it was not, and some teachers applied the standards one way and other teachers the other way. Eau Claire, Wisconsin, is very clear that the standards are year-end standards, while Douglas County is equally clear that the standard is what is expected at the time of the report card. If you adopt the Eau Claire approach, you have to educate parents to understand that there will be very few students proficient in anything until the third quarter at the earliest. If you adopt the Douglas County approach, the progression expected from the first report card to the second, and so on, must be clear.

Achievement, Growth, and Progress

The performance standards just described are about achievement—at which *absolute* level is the student achieving? For example, "Douglas is proficient on persuasive writing at a fifth-grade level." "Jeff is approaching proficiency in mathematics problem solving at a ninth-grade level." Achievement is related to growth, but growth is relative, and the point of reference is the student—how much has the student grown from a stated time in the past? Progress, which is related to achievement and growth, is relative, and the point of reference is proficiency—how much has the student progressed to or toward proficiency over a period of time? It is possible that a student could be making significant growth while making limited progress at a low level of achievement, or that a student could be making little growth and no progress at a high level of achievement.

It is rare that there is confusion between achievement and growth, but there is often confusion between achievement and progress. For example, many schools and districts label the first report card of the school year as a progress report, but the report has grades on it, so it is an achievement report; if it were really a progress report, it would have a different set of symbols with descriptors that are appropriate to progress. Generally, achievement should be seen as the base for grades, while growth and progress should be part of the narrative and comments section of each report card. El Monte City School District in California, however, reports effectively on achievement and progress on the same report card by using the symbols and descriptors shown in figures 4.3 and 4.4.

III. Academic Achievement

The Academic Achievement grade is an indicator of a student's mastery of grade-level Power Standards. Students demonstrate what they know, understand, and can do as measured through multiple assessments and observations.

4 Exemplary (exceeds)	3 Proficient (meets)	2 Partially Proficient (approaching)	1 Nonproficient (below)

4 Exemplary: The student demonstrates mastery, with excellence, of the grade-level standards with relative ease and consistency, and often exceeds the cognitive level of the standards. The student applies and extends the key concepts, processes, and skills. The student is working at grade level yet at a higher level of Bloom's taxonomy. There is no mark of 4+ or 4−.

3 Proficient: The student demonstrates mastery of the grade-level standards at the cognitive level the standard is written. The student consistently grasps and applies key concepts, processes, and skills with limited errors. There is no mark of 3+ or 3−.

2 Partially Proficient: The student demonstrates mastery of some grade-level standards. The student inconsistently grasps and applies some of the key concepts, processes, and skills with significant errors. There is no mark of 2+ or 2−.

1 Nonproficient: The student has not demonstrated mastery of grade-level standards and is not yet performing at grade level. There is no mark of 1+ or 1−.

Source: El Monte City School District, El Monte, California. Used with permission.

Figure 4.3: El Monte City School District achievement reporting.

IV. Progress Toward Proficiency

These marks represent the measurement of a student's growth toward and attainment of mastery of each district Power Standard in reading, writing, and math. Progress is measured by a variety of evidence, which includes quality standards-aligned assessments, portfolios, and other multiple measures.

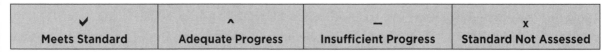

✔ Meets Standard	^ Adequate Progress	— Insufficient Progress	x Standard Not Assessed

✔ **Meets or Exceeds Standard**—The student has mastered the entire standard. Unless reassessment indicates otherwise, the ✔ is repeated in subsequent trimesters.

^ **Adequate Progress (used first and second trimester only)**—Based on what has been taught and assessed, the student is on track to master the standard by the end of the year. This symbol is not used in the third trimester.

— **Insufficient Progress**—Based on what has been taught and assessed, the student has not demonstrated that s/he is on track to master the standard by the end of the year. For the third trimester, this symbol represents that the student has NOT demonstrated mastery of the standard in its entirety.

x **Standard Not Assessed (used first and second trimester only)**—Standard has not been taught and/or measured to date. This symbol is not used in the third trimester.

Source: El Monte City School District, El Monte, California. Used with permission.

Figure 4.4: El Monte City School District progress reporting.

Generally, achievement should be seen as the base for grades, while growth and progress should be part of the narrative and comments section of each report card.

Further information about El Monte's approach to standards-based reporting can be found at the El Monte City School District website (www.emcsd.org; El Monte City School District, n.d.).

Criterion- or Norm-Referenced Assessment?

A criterion-referenced assessment is defined as follows:

> An assessment where an individual's performance is compared to a specific learning objective or performance standard and not to the performance of other students. Criterion-referenced assessment tells us how well students are performing on specific goals or standards rather than just telling how their performance compares to a norm group of students nationally or locally. In criterion-referenced assessments, it is possible that none, or all, of the examinees will reach a particular goal or performance standard. (North Central Regional Educational Laboratory, n.d.a)

The National Center for Research on Evaluation, Standards, and Student Testing defines *norm-referenced assessment* as follows:

> An assessment where student performance or performances are compared to a larger group. Usually the larger group or 'norm group' is a national sample representing a wide and diverse cross-section of students. Students, schools, districts, or even states are then compared or rank-ordered in relation to the norm group. The purpose of a norm-referenced assessment is usually to sort students and not to measure achievement toward some criterion of performance. (North Central Regional Educational Laboratory, n.d.b)

These definitions make the differences between criterion and norm referencing very clear. In standards-based schools, where our objective is, at least, proficiency for all, it is essential that principals be clear that we have to be criterion-referenced, not norm-referenced, because in criterion-referenced assessment we are trying to find the level of performance of each student, and any distribution of scores and performance is possible. Norm referencing is about the distribution of scores whatever the level of performance, and there is a preset distribution of scores that may tell us nothing about the level of achievement. If we have a strong group of students, they may have quite high levels of performance that fall near the bottom of the distribution and so would receive a low score or grade, but if we had a weak group, students with quite low levels of performance might be at the top of the distribution and would get a high score or grade.

I doubt that this was ever an issue in the early years of elementary schools, but it has sometimes been an issue in upper elementary and middle schools, so *principals* of schools with grades 4 to 8 must ensure that no teacher is allowing anything like the bell curve to creep into grading practices.

Policy and Procedures

In addition to having high-quality performance standards that are shared with and understood by all stakeholders, it is essential that principals ensure that all teachers in their school understand and operate within state or provincial and district policies and procedures. One of the best ways to ensure that this happens is to develop school-level assessment, grading, and reporting policies and procedures, because doing so requires the principal and the teachers (and often some parents and community members) to examine state or provincial and district policies, with the objective of selecting the aspects that are most significant for their school. An example of a district policy can be found in appendix A; appendix B contains a school policy from the same district. You might find it a worthwhile exercise to read these policies and compare them with your own. You could do this on your own, with your leadership team, or with your whole faculty. You will notice that the district policy is very general, and while the school policy is more specific—and both contain important and useful directions for teachers—neither provides specific guidance with regard to grading.

Other districts provide more direction for teachers with regard to grading in their policies. An example is provided by Bay District Schools in Florida. We have already seen (page 6) the Bay District Schools Classroom Assessment Guiding Principles. For each of the principles, Bay District has developed guidelines that have been adopted as district policy by the school board. The guidelines for principle 4—"Grading is fair, consistent, and meaningful"—are shown in figure 4.5. These guidelines provide clear guidance and direction for teachers, and when used effectively, will lead to grades that are consistent across the district.

Guideline 4.1: Teachers determine grades based on individual achievement of content standards.

- The teacher carefully designs assessments to closely align with the learning target.
- The teacher determines achievement of standards for each individual student. Group scores are not used for individual grading.

Guideline 4.2: Teachers inform students about grading criteria and methods used for determining grades.

- At the beginning of the lesson or unit, the teacher explains the grading criteria with the students.
  + The criteria are specific and related to the targeted benchmark(s).
  + If possible, the students are given copies of the criteria.
- The teacher should explain the assessment method that will be used to determine the student's grade (essay questions, open response, open book, performance, and so on).

Guideline 4.3: Teachers use predetermined and consistent grading procedures in the same courses and across grade levels.

- Teachers of the same course and/or grade level meet and compare assessments and student results on a regular basis.
  + They have a common understanding of what mastery of their course standards looks like based on district expectations.
  + They share exemplars, anchors, assessments, and scoring tools as appropriate to increase their understanding of what quality student work should reflect.
- Teachers of the same course and/or grade level meet and decide upon such issues as:
  + Weighting to accurately reflect student mastery of content
  + Using most recent data in some circumstances
  + Using the median or mode rather than the mean in some circumstances

Guideline 4.4: Teachers use evidence from summative assessments to determine all or a major part of the grade, placing more emphasis on the most recent cumulative knowledge and skills, when appropriate. Summative grades should not be significantly impacted by formative work/grades.

- The teacher determines final grades based primarily or entirely on summative assessments, since this evidence represents achievement after having had the chance to learn in a low-stakes environment.

- When assessing cumulative knowledge, performance, and skills, such as writing ability, math facts, problem solving, reading comprehension, and phonics skills, the teacher assesses and records information throughout the term placing more emphasis on the most recent demonstration of student learning, when appropriate.

- When determining and reporting term grades for such knowledge, performance, and skills, the teacher analyzes the recorded information to determine the most consistent and highest level of achievement.

  + Example: At the beginning of the term, the student could count from 1 to 5. By the end of the term, the student could count consistently from 1 to 50. Rather than average all attempts throughout the term, the teacher reported the more recent information as measured against the learning target. If the target was counting to 50, then the student exhibited mastery and earned an A.

  + Example: Over the course of the term, the student made the following scores on timed writing practice, using the FCAT Writing Assessment rubric for the scoring tool: 1, 2, 2, 3, 2, 3, 3, 3. Based on this information, the teacher used the score of 3 when reporting writing achievement because a 3 represents the most recent and consistent level of achievement.

Guideline 4.5: Teachers use the most appropriate measure of central tendency (mean, median, mode) to determine a student's most fair, meaningful, and accurate grade.

- Teachers strive to assign grades that are an accurate reflection of student mastery of standards.

- Course and subject grades are supported by a body of classroom assessment evidence that substantiates teacher professional judgments.

Guideline 4.6: Teachers provide makeup opportunities for students who miss a summative assessment due to reasons approved by the district as stated in School Board Policy 7.104.

- The teacher arranges to meet the student during a planning period or before/after school to make up a summative assessment.

Guideline 4.7: The determination of grades is not related to behaviors, such as motivation, participation, compliance, attendance, and attitude.

- A conduct/behavior grade will not affect an academic grade as stated in School Board Policy 8.201.

Source: Bay District Schools, Panama City Beach, Florida. Used with permission.

Figure 4.5: Guidelines for principle 4—grading is fair, consistent, and meaningful.

Given this level of detail in district policy, the school policy at Deer Point Elementary School in Bay District is very simple and concise:

- How a teacher grades must be communicated to students and their parents.

- Each teacher will have a "grading policy," which clearly depicts the criteria and methods used to obtain student grades.

- Deer Point faculty members will implement quality assessment and grading practices as outlined in the district's Classroom Assessment Guidelines.

- Grades are to be a clear depiction of individual student learning of standards. (L. Willis, personal communication, February 24, 2012)

As noted in the introduction, within the limits set by the other levels, teachers should develop and make available for administrators and parents the procedures that will be used in their classrooms. These should be fairly concise documents that focus on the parts of state and district policies that are most significant for the grade level and subjects being taught. When there is more than one teacher teaching a grade level or a subject, these classroom-level procedures should be developed and communicated collaboratively, not independently. An example of teacher and classroom procedures from Bay District Schools is provided in figure 4.6.

Breakfast Point Academy
Sixth-Grade Advanced World History Syllabus

Welcome

Welcome to sixth-grade advanced world history! I look forward to a great school year ahead filled with fun and learning. This letter is to provide both the student and the parent with some general information about how to succeed in this social studies course.

Course Objectives

Sixth-grade advanced social studies is a course that focuses on world history, as well as historical inquiry. Students will have the opportunity to investigate and explore objectives outlined in the Florida Sunshine State Standards for social studies. This will be accomplished through a combination of learning methods such as hands-on activities and labs, cooperative learning groups, discussions, note taking, journal writing, and group and individual practice. Students will utilize historical inquiry to identify and solve problems, work cooperatively to achieve common goals, make connections between historical concepts and current events, connect history and the modern world using computers and other technology, and make historical connections through the research and writing process. Students will be involved in cross-curricular learning units utilizing fiction and nonfiction texts and novel studies.

Advanced World History

Honors/advanced courses offer scaffolded learning opportunities for students to develop the critical skills of analysis, synthesis, and evaluation in a more rigorous and reflective academic setting. Students are empowered to perform at higher levels as they engage in the following: analyzing historical documents and supplementary readings, working in the context of thematically categorized information, becoming proficient in note taking, participating in Socratic seminars/discussions, emphasizing free-response and document-based writing, contrasting opposing viewpoints, solving problems, and so on. Students will develop and demonstrate their skills through participation in a capstone and/or extended research-based paper/project (for example, history fair, participatory citizenship project, mock congressional hearing, projects for competitive evaluation, investment portfolio contests, or other teacher-directed projects).

History Fair Project/Participation

Students will create a history fair project that they may place in the Breakfast Point History Fair. Students will engage in this research project utilizing primary and secondary sources. Project due dates and expectations will be sent out in November, and final projects will be due in January. Ample class time will be given for completion of the project, but some aspects of the project may need to be completed at home.

Students have five different types of product options for their projects: 3D exhibit, historical research paper, documentary project, webpage, or live performance. The theme for this year's history fair is Revolution, Reaction, and Reform in History.

Grading Policy

Formative Assessment—10% The use of formative assessment is to guide instruction and provide students with feedback. Formative assessment is used to change instruction and learning activities to meet individual student needs. This includes but is not limited to class work, written comments, group discussions, observations, questioning, a variety of products, self-evaluation, and quizzes.

Summative Assessment—90% Summative assessment will be graded for accuracy. The use of summative assessment is to show proficiency of the learning target. Summative assessments are used to evaluate student progress of standards and identify areas that need additional attention. This includes but is not limited to tests, projects, products, and presentations.

If summative work is not completed and there is insufficient evidence available to assess the standard, students will receive an *I*, or incomplete grade, on their report card. Students may have additional opportunities to show mastery of the learning target. Alternative assessments based on specific student needs may be necessary.

All makeup work (work assigned while a student is absent) must be turned in to the teacher within five days of returning to school. (This is Bay District policy.) It is the student's responsibility to request makeup work.

Classroom Expectations

- Be responsible.
- Be respectful.
- Be prompt.
- Be prepared.

All students can experience success in school with effort, focus, and positive communication.

All assignments and due dates will be posted on my classroom website. Please check this often for information regarding your student's class work and projects.

Sincerely,

Alana Simmons

Source: Breakfast Point Academy, Bay District Schools, Panama City Beach, Florida. Used with permission.

Figure 4.6: Syllabus and grading procedures for Ms. Simmons's class.

Principals have a responsibility to ensure that teachers are implementing state or provincial, district, and school policies, so it is desirable that they collect the classroom assessment procedures documents from all their teachers and provide them with feedback. In evaluating teachers' classroom procedures, Stephen Friedman suggests the following guidelines for principals:

- Understand the teacher's perspective.
- Beware of traits that do not measure achievement.
- Consider the quality of the grading information.
- Think about the role of homework.

- Expect teachers to use numbers.

- Know how the numbers should be combined.

- Encourage consumerism.

- Demand fairness.

- Hold teachers accountable. (Friedman, 1998)

Summary

It should never have been acceptable for students who are achieving at the same level to get different grades, but it must be completely unacceptable in a standards-based system. Making grades accurate and meaningful contributes to consistency, but in order to ensure that grades are consistent, it is essential that principals have in place clear, well-written, criterion-referenced performance standards that describe achievement using a limited number of levels related to proficiency, not points or percentages. It is also essential that principals develop school policies that "nest" within district and state or provincial policies and that they require each teacher, or group of teachers teaching the same grade level or subject, to have classroom and subject grading procedures that are shared with parents, students, and the principal.

CONCLUSION

I have made the case that grades need to be supportive of learning, as well as accurate, meaningful, and consistent, and that traditional grading practices have frequently resulted in grades that do not meet these standards. It is no longer acceptable to have "broken grades" in standards-based systems, where the objective is proficiency for all. Grading is not—and should never have been—a private practice. Teachers are not independent contractors. Schools and districts must have policies and procedures and demand that all teachers follow them regardless of their personal preferences and beliefs. The essential role of principals is to support moving grading from being a private practice to a shared practice. Being mindful of the seven Ps identified in figure I.1 (page 3) and operating within the nested hierarchy of policy and procedures identified in figure I.2 (page 10), principals must be strong leaders for grading that is supportive of learning, accurate, meaningful, and consistent. In this endeavor, you must recognize that you may run into significant opposition from some parents and teachers who do not like change and do not like to see the status quo challenged. You must be steadfast in presenting the case against many traditional grading practices and presenting the case for standards-based grading.

In this 21st century, when all schools are supposed to be standards based (or outcomes based, expectations based, or, generically, learning goals based), to move toward focusing on learning for all students, there are two givens that are not open for discussion and eight musts about which—while there may be discussion of the details and implementation—there should be no discussion about the principles involved. Principals have to ensure the givens are in place, and that their school is moving forward—even if in very small steps—on the musts.

The two givens are *quality assessment* (doing it right) and *student involvement* (using it well). There can be no disagreement that assessment has to be high in quality and that every teacher must know the differences between sound and unsound assessment practices. When, and only when, assessment is high in quality does everyone involved have the accurate, useful information needed to improve learning and instruction. Also, there can be no disagreement that learners control their own learning, and so they must be actively involved in the learning and assessment process. The ability to self-assess, reflect, and set goals is critical to successful learning whether you are five, twelve, or sixteen. Students need opportunities to learn how to do these things, get feedback on how they are doing, and become skilled, independent, self-directed learners.

The eight musts are:

1. Curriculum, instruction, assessment grading, and reporting must be standards based. Students and parents must receive profiles of student performance, and there should be no grades for overall performance in a subject for kindergarten to grade 8.

2. Performance standards must be descriptions of a limited number of levels based on proficiency, and there should be no percentages used in grading.

3. Achievement must be separated from behaviors on expanded-format report cards.

4. There should be no mark penalties for late work, missing work, academic dishonesty, or absences.

5. Grades must be determined primarily from summative assessments.

6. Formative assessment should be no mark, comment only, with homework having little or no part of grades.

7. When learning is cumulative and developmental (as most learning is), the more recent evidence must be emphasized in the determination of a grade.

8. Grades must be determined, not calculated: "number crunching" should be limited, and there should be no use of the mean or of zeros.

Principals should see that their objective is that students and parents will no longer ask, "What can be done to improve the grade?" but instead will ask, "What can be done to improve the learning?" I believe we can get to this point by, as Wiliam (2011) says, "design[ing] smarter grading systems that provide accurate information about student achievement while supporting student learning" (p. 123). He says that "we need classroom assessment systems that are designed primarily to support learning and deal in data that are recorded at a level that is useful for teachers, students, and parents in determining where students are in their learning. Such fine-scale evidence can always be aggregated for summative reporting" (2011, p. 124).

Traditional grading has commonly led to students and parents who are hooked on grades (and honor rolls, and class rank, and bumper stickers boasting that their child is a high-achieving student), but if you take the approaches described in this book, we can get them to understand that school is about learning, not grades. This will be made easier if we don't get children hooked on grades in the first place. One way to do this is to have students understand the assessment and grading process. This was done brilliantly by Kathryn Burnett-Klebart, a third-grade teacher at Allen Frear Elementary School in the Caesar Rodney School District in Delaware. When working with her students in social studies on the Bill of Rights, they developed a grading bill of rights (figure C.1). I think we would really move forward if principals encouraged all teachers to do this with their students, and so I give the final words in this book to Kathryn and her students.

Just as our country has a Bill of Rights, you as students, in this classroom, have grading rights.

First, you have the right to know what you are being graded on, your third-grade standards.

Second, you have the right to have practice time, or formative assessments, before game time, the summative assessments.

Third, you have the right to know your stars and stairs without embarrassment.

Fourth, you have the right to make up any missed work.

Fifth, you have the right to not have any grade penalty for being absent.

Sixth, you have the freedom to ask questions about a standard or grade.

Seventh, you have the right to know the standard, or target, before the lesson begins.

Eighth, you have the right to a fair hearing if at any time you disagree with a grade.

Ninth, you have the right to receive detailed feedback on your practice, or formative assessments.

Tenth, you have the freedom to progress toward the standards, or targets, at your own pace!

Source: Kathryn Burnett-Klebart, Third-Grade Teacher, Allen Frear Elementary School, Caesar Rodney School District, Dover, Delaware. Reprinted with permission.

Figure C.1: Student grading rights.

APPENDIX A

Des Moines, Iowa, Public School District Policies

Series 600, Code 603.3: Curriculum Evaluation

Regular evaluation of the total curriculum is necessary to ensure that the written and delivered curriculum is having the desired effect for students.

Curriculum evaluation refers to an ongoing process of collecting, analyzing, synthesizing, and interpreting information to aid in understanding what students know and can do. It refers to the full range of information gathered in the School District to evaluate (make judgments about) student learning and program effectiveness in each content area.

Curriculum evaluation must be based on information gathered from a comprehensive assessment system that is designed for accountability and committed to the concept that all students will achieve at high levels, is standards-based, and informs decisions that impact significant and sustainable improvements in teaching and student learning.

The superintendent shall be responsible for curriculum evaluation and for determining the most effective way of ensuring that assessment activities are integrated into instructional practices as part of school improvement with a particular focus on improving teaching and learning. A curriculum framework shall describe the procedures that will be followed to establish an evaluation process that can efficiently and effectively evaluate the total curriculum. This framework will, at a minimum, describe the procedures for the following curriculum evaluation activities:

- Identify specific purposes for assessing student learning.

- Develop a comprehensive assessment plan.

- Select/develop assessment tools and scoring procedures that are valid and reliable.

- Identify procedures for collecting assessment data.

- Identify procedures for analyzing and interpreting information and drawing conclusions based on the data (including analysis of the performance of various sub-groups of students).

- Identify procedures for establishing at least three levels of performance (specific to the content standard and the assessment tool when appropriate) to assist in determining whether students have achieved at a satisfactory level (at least two levels describe performance that is proficient or advanced and at least one level describes students who are not yet performing at the proficient level).

- Identify procedures for using assessment information to determine long-range and annual improvement goals.

- Identify procedures for using assessment information in making decisions focused on improving teaching and learning (data-based decision making).

- Provide support to staff in using data to make instructional decisions.

- Define procedures for regular and clear communication about assessment results to the various internal and external publics (mandatory for communication about students receiving special education services).

- Define data reporting procedures.

- Verify that assessment tools are fair for all students and are consistent with all state and federal mandates.

- Verify that assessment tools measure the curriculum that is written and delivered.

- Identify procedures for deciding when multiple assessment measures are necessary for making good decisions and drawing appropriate conclusions about student learning.

- Identify roles and responsibilities of key groups.

- Involve staff, parents, students, and community members in curriculum evaluation.

- Ensure participation of eligible students receiving special education services in district-wide assessments.

It shall be the responsibility of the superintendent to keep the board apprised of curriculum evaluation activities [and] the progress of each content area related to curriculum evaluation activities, and to develop administrative regulations for curriculum evaluation including recommendations to the board.

Series 600, Code 608: Evaluation and Testing

Des Moines Independent Community School District will provide a variety of unbiased assessments of student academic growth. DMPS [Des Moines Public Schools] will also provide a district-wide testing program. Specialized testing will also be undertaken as part of unique, individual student instructional requirements and educational services.

The administration shall submit evaluation reports to the Board of Directors concerning programs and curricular services through its monitoring report schedule in order to provide timely information about student achievement.

The Des Moines School District is committed to ensuring the integrity of the information obtained from the use of educational assessments. This policy is intended to apply to two assessments in particular, ITBS/ITED and District Criterion-Reference Tests (CRT).

The purpose of this policy is to ensure that assessment results are truly representative of the achievement of students in our district. It is also our intent to create awareness of the potential negative impact that inappropriate assessment practices might produce (to outline processes to be followed) and to identify the potential consequences of violating the policy. If test scores become questionable because of inappropriate practices in either preparing students or in administering tests, the meaning of the scores will be distorted and their value for their original purpose will be diminished or lost.

Appointment of District Assessment Team

The district shall appoint a District Assessment Team who may delegate responsibility for testing-related functions to one or more school Test Coordinators. The District Assessment Coordinator is responsible for storing materials from Iowa Test Programs in a secure area with restricted access both prior to and after the testing period.

Consequences of Policy Violations

If a violation of this policy occurs as determined by the Superintendent and following an investigation of allegations of irregularities, the Superintendent shall determine whether the integrity of the testing program has been jeopardized, whether some or all of the test results are invalidated, and whether a teacher or administrator has violated the Code of Administrative Conduct Chapter 25.

A staff member found to have committed testing irregularities shall be subject to discipline in accordance with law and Board policy. If the staff member is a licensee of the Board of Educational Examiners, the Superintendent shall make a timely report to that Board.

Reports of students cheating on assessments shall be submitted to the building principal for investigation and disciplinary procedures.

If the Superintendent believes that assessment results are invalid, the Superintendent shall make a timely report to the Iowa Department of Education.

Series 600, Code 643: Student Progress Reports and Conferences

Students will receive progress reports. In addition, parent-teacher conferences will be held twice annually to keep parents informed about student performance.

Parents, principals, teachers, counselors, and other administrators may request a conference for students in grades kindergarten through twelve in addition to the scheduled conference time. Parents and students are encouraged to discuss the student's progress or other matters with the student's teacher and to utilize the District's Infinite Campus system to help stay informed on these types of issues.

Source: Des Moines Independent Community Public Schools, Des Moines, Iowa. Used with permission.

APPENDIX B

Hubbell Elementary School (a Des Moines Public School) Assessment Policy

This assessment policy was written collaboratively by the Hubbell Assessment Committee. It will be shared with all stakeholders and reviewed annually.

At Hubbell Elementary School, we believe assessment is an integral part of the instructional cycle and is essential for learners constructing meaning. It allows for the collection and analysis of information and gives insight into the teaching and learning happening in the school. Students will have the opportunity to illustrate their knowledge of content and skills through demonstrations of their understanding of concepts and their ability to transfer that learning to real-world situations using authentic assessments. A variety of models should be used to reach the various learning styles of all students. The Hubbell community believes that assessment drives the improvement of the PYP [Primary Years Program]. It is crucial to assess not only the product of the inquiry, but also the process.

Pre-Assessment

Pre-assessments are used at the beginning of each unit of inquiry to inform instruction and plan for differentiation based on prior knowledge and/or learning styles. These assessment tools give valuable information into what to teach, how to teach, and how to connect it to students' interests and talents, as well as uncover any misconceptions.

Formative Assessment

Formative assessments are used throughout the unit to guide instruction and can be done formally or informally. They provide quick, detailed, and understandable feedback for students. They allow time for students and teachers to make self-adjustments to teaching and learning. Well-designed learning experiences as well as checklists, student-created rubrics, observations, and anecdotal notes are some examples of formative assessments used at Hubbell Elementary School.

In addition, one formative assessment per unit will be created and administered collaboratively at every grade level. . . .

Summative Assessment

Summative assessments are used to measure student understanding of the central idea. Authentic summative assessments prompt students to action and communicate learning to parents, students, and teachers. Various examples, or models, are shown to students at the beginning of the unit, and the criteria for the assessment are defined prior to embarking on the learning. A common rubric is used for grade levels to allow for consistency in evaluation and collaboration.

Self-Assessment and Reflection

Hubbell is striving to create reflective learners who have the capacity to self-assess their academic progress. Teacher modeling is crucial to creating this reflective environment. Students are given ample opportunity to reflect on their learning during the course of each unit. In addition, students will self-assess their knowledge, development of the transdisciplinary skills, and evidence of the learner profile traits and attitudes at the conclusion of each unit. These reflections will be developed by grade level teams and may vary according to student age and ability. In addition, a reflection of all the learner profile traits will be completed for fall and spring conferences in grades 2–5. Grade 1 will complete this reflection for spring conferences only.

Portfolios

Portfolios are used to celebrate student learning through the collection of student work. They document student growth over time including successes, higher-order thinking, creativity, and reflection. Portfolios are also used as a communication tool between students, teachers, and parents.

Protocol for portfolios:

- ☐ 3 ring binder

- ☐ Storage in classroom

- ☐ Used by students and teachers to document learning

- ☐ Move with the student from kindergarten to fifth grade

- ☐ Include the summative assessment from each unit of inquiry

- ☐ Include the self-assessment from each unit of inquiry

- ☐ Include one student-selected piece from each unit of inquiry with reflection (each selection will include the transdisciplinary theme, central idea, and date)

- ☐ Include a reflection of all learner profile traits—twice per year (2nd–5th), once per year (1st)

- ☐ Include an end-of-year reflection from art, music, PE, and Spanish

Mandatory Assessments

The DSM district requires various assessments for literacy and math as follows:

- PA [Phonological Awareness] Profile (K–2)

- Reading BRI [Basic Reading Inventory] (K–3) and ARI [Analytic Reading Inventory] (4–5)

- Literacy Theme Tests twice per year (2–5)

- Writing Assessment once per year (1–5)

- Math CRT [Criterion-Referenced Test]

- ITBS [Iowa Test of Basic Skills (now called Iowa Assessments)]

Reporting on Student Learning

Conferences: Hubbell holds two three-way conferences each year, in the fall and spring. Students will reflect on all ten learner profile attributes to share with parents at conferences. Student portfolios will also be shared at this time.

Additional reporting: The DSM School District requires report cards for Terms 2, 3, 5, and 6. In addition to these report cards, various products [in] all subject areas will be sent home throughout the units and at the conclusion of each unit. The Hubbell newsletter is sent home monthly with curriculum updates for parents as well.

Upcoming: Hubbell is looking into changing the conference schedule as well as the district report card.

Source: Des Moines Independent Community Public Schools. Used with permission.

APPENDIX C

Lawrence Public Schools, Kansas, Grade 3 Report Card

Student: 2011–2012

Third-Grade Homeroom: Principal:

Class: **READING, THIRD GRADE**

Teacher:

Vocabulary	
Uses a variety of strategies to decode words	
Determines meaning of unknown words through the use of text clues, word structure, use of dictionary	
Fluency	
Demonstrates appropriate pace, phrasing, and rhythm (fluency) to orally read all text types	
Comprehension	
Distinguishes between narrative, expository, persuasive, and technical texts and the purpose for reading	
Understands the purpose of text features (title, table of contents, etc.)	
Identifies topic, main idea, and supporting details	
Identifies text structures (sequence, compare/contrast, cause/effect, problem/solution, description/definition)	
Identifies story elements in narrative (setting, characters, plot, etc.)	
Makes connections with characters in literature	
Makes inferences and draws conclusions	

Class: **WRITING, THIRD GRADE**

Teacher:

Writing	
Uses the writing process to produce written work in all text types	
Writes in narrative style (diaries, biographies, plays, short stories)	
Writes in expository style (journal articles, informational articles, how-to, research summaries)	
Writes in technical style (instructions, contracts, manuals, procedures)	
Uses six-trait model: ideas and content, organization, voice, word choice, sentence fluency, conventions	
Writes legibly (presentation)	
Writes letters correctly in daily work	

Class: **RESEARCH, THIRD GRADE**

Teacher:

Research	
Uses multiple sources in researching a topic	
Takes notes in key words or phrases	
Constructs simple bibliography	

Class: **MATH, THIRD GRADE**

Teacher:

Number Sense and Computation	
Reads and writes numbers from tenth place to 10,000	
Uses place value to write, count, order, and compare numbers	
Uses a variety of methods to estimate quantities	
Knows and uses basic facts efficiently (addition, subtraction, multiplication, and division)	
Explains and performs computations in a variety of situations	
Recognizes and uses money representations	
Recognizes and uses fractions and decimals	
Knows and uses problem-solving skills	
Learns and uses vocabulary related to math concepts	
Algebra, Patterns, and Functions	
Recognizes, extends, and creates patterns (number, visual word, etc.)	
Uses symbols to solve equations	
Determines the rule for functions and input/output and t-tables (+/-)	
Knows and uses problem-solving skills	
Learns and uses vocabulary related to math concepts	

Statistics, Data, and Probability	
Uses probability to make predictions	
Collects, organizes, displays, and interprets data	
Recognizes and uses statistical values (minimum/maximum, range, mode, median)	
Knows and uses problem-solving skills	
Learns and uses vocabulary related to math concepts	
Geometry and Measurement	
Recognizes and describes geometric shapes	
Uses both standard and nonstandard measurement tools and applies measurement strategies	
Reads, calculates, and tells time to the minute	
Recognizes and describes a single transformation (flip, slide, turn)	
Finds points on a vertical or horizontal number line	
Knows and uses problem-solving skills	
Learns and uses vocabulary related to math concepts	

Class: SCIENCE AND HEALTH, THIRD GRADE

Teacher:

Science and Health	
Follows the steps in scientific inquiry to make observations and apply the scientific process	
Uses tools and technology effectively	
Collects data, makes decisions based on findings, actively participates in investigations (experiments/labs)	
Learns concepts related to science content and communicates using scientific vocabulary	
Learns concepts related to health content and communicates using appropriate health vocabulary	
Understands effective strategies for personal safety and health	

Class: SOCIAL STUDIES, THIRD GRADE

Teacher:

Social Studies	
Understands the basic purpose of local government	
Understands basic economic concepts	
Uses basic geography skills	
Connects the Lawrence community and local residents to Kansas history	
Looks at local resources to explain the origin of Lawrence	

Class: **SUCCESSFUL LEARNER BEHAVIOR, THIRD GRADE**

Teacher:

Successful Learner Behavior	
Shows acceptance of others and ideas	
Respects others (teachers, substitutes, paras, student teachers, peers, etc.)	
Actively listens	
Responds appropriately to feedback	
Uses materials purposefully and respectfully	
Follows directions	
Uses organizational strategies, organizes classroom materials/personal belongings	
Uses time efficiently and constructively	
Strives to produce quality work	
Completes tasks on time (classwork/homework)	
Manages transitions and changes in routine	
Exercises self-control	
Accepts responsibility for behavior	
Works quietly and stays on task	
Uses cooperation skills (whole group, small group, partners)	

Class: **ART, THIRD GRADE**

Teacher:

Art	
Explains the difference between various techniques*	
Identifies the elements in works of art (color, space)*	
Practices using key principles (repetition/rhythm/pattern, eye movement/composition, balance)	
Categorizes works based on the use of subject, symbols, and ideas*	
Creates art that uses art techniques from other cultures	
Restates the narrative depicted in an art work	
Defines and uses vocabulary appropriate to the discussion of art works	
Explains the difference between a reproduction and an original work of art*	
Successful learner behaviors: exhibits self-control in order to learn	
Successful learner behaviors: follows rules and procedures	
Successful learner behaviors: actively listens and watches during instruction	
Successful learner behaviors: applies effort to work, attends to detail, and participates in learning activities	

* Intermediate standards

Class: **MUSIC, THIRD GRADE**

Teacher:

Music	
Sings a short, age-appropriate song on pitch and in rhythm with a steady beat	
Performs on classroom instruments accurately her/his part, while other students perform contrasting parts	
Creates, arranges, and performs a short instrumental piece within specified guidelines	
Correctly identifies rhythmic patterns in 3/4 and 4/4 meter using whole, half, dotted half, quarter, and eighth notes and corresponding rests given an aural example	
Identifies and sings known pitches (*do, re, mi, so,* and *la*) in a notated example accurately	
Uses appropriate vocabulary when describing similarities and differences of musical examples	
Identifies criteria to evaluate a composition	

Class: **PHYSICAL EDUCATION, THIRD GRADE**

Teacher:

Physical Education	
Demonstrates competency in motor skills and movement patterns needed to perform a variety of physical activities	
Demonstrates body awareness and control as it applies to the learning and understanding of physical activities	
Achieves and maintains a health-enhancing level of physical fitness	
Successful learner behaviors: exhibits voluntary effort and participation in classroom activities	
Successful learner behaviors: exercises self-control	

Grade Mark Legend	
S	Successfully meets academic (or learner behavior) expectations. Evidence of most recent work demonstrates that the learning goals are fully and consistently met.
M	Making progress: Partially meets academic (or learner behavior) expectations. Evidence of most recent work demonstrates more than half of the learning goals are fully and consistently met.
T	Targeted for growth in order to meet academic (or learner behavior) expectations: Evidence of most recent work demonstrates only a few of the learning goals are met or partially met.
E	Excels: Consistently goes beyond academic (or learner behavior) expectations. Evidence of most recent work demonstrates that the learning goals are fully and consistently met.
S*	Successfully meets academic (or learner behavior) expectations with work modified and/or additional support provided (teacher, resource staff, etc.).
M*	Making progress: Partially meets academic (or learner behavior) expectations with work modified and/or additional support provided (teacher, resource staff, etc.).
T*	Targeted for growth in order to meet academic (or learner behavior) expectations with work modified and/or additional support provided (teacher, resource staff, etc.).

	Grade Mark Legend *(continued)*	
E*	Excels: Consistently goes beyond academic (or learner behavior) expectations with work modified and/or additional support provided (teacher, resource staff, etc.).	
I	Incomplete: Insufficient evidence to report achievement.	
	Blank space: Standards not assessed during the trimester.	

* Additional support provided (teacher, para-educator, etc.)

Source: Lawrence Public Schools, Lawrence, Kansas. Used with permission.

Lawrence Public Schools, Kansas, Grade 6 Report Card

Student: 2011–2012

Sixth Grade

Class: **Advisory 6**

Teacher:

Advisory: Comments	

Class: **Art 6**

Teacher:

Art Standards/Indicators	
Value—Demonstrates the ability to apply value to create the illusion of 3D on a 2D surface	
Color—Manipulates color to create intermediate colors, tints, and shades	
3D—Creates a 3D work of art that shows competency and craftsmanship	
Draw—Demonstrates ability to draw from observation	
Perspective—Applies the rules of linear perspective in a work of art	
Communicate—Analyzes and communicates about works of art	
Successful Learner Behaviors	
Responds appropriately to others, ideas, and feedback	
Uses cooperation and communication skills	
Exercises self-control	
Uses materials purposefully and respectfully	
Uses organizational strategies	
Actively listens, follows directions	
Stays on task, completes tasks on time	
Strives to produce quality work	

Class: **Guided Studies 6**

Teacher:

Guided Studies: Comments	

Class: **Language Arts 6**

Teacher:

Language Arts: Reading Standards/Indicators	
Uses a variety of strategies to expand vocabulary	
Reads fluently in all text types	
Identifies story elements of narrative text (setting, characters, plot, etc.)	
Identifies and analyzes how text structures support comprehension of text (compare/contract, cause/effect, sequence, etc.)	
Determines the topic, main idea, and supporting details	
Comprehends narrative, expository, persuasive, and technical texts for purpose of reading	
Identifies evidence that supports conclusions in persuasive text	
Distinguishes between fact and fiction	
Understands and identifies text features (title, table of contents, boldface, italics, etc.)	
Writing Standards/Indicators	
Uses the writing process to produce written work in all text types	
Understands and identifies text features (title, table of contents, boldface, italics, etc.)	
Writes in narrative style (diaries, biographies, plays, short stories, etc.)	
Writes in expository style (journal articles, informational articles, how-to, research summaries, etc.)	
Writes in technical style (instructions, contracts, manuals, procedures, etc.)	
Writes in persuasive style (reviews, advertisements, proposals, editorials, position papers, etc.)	
Uses six-trait model: ideas and content, organization, voice, word choice, sentence fluency, conventions	
Writes legibly (presentation)	
Research Standards/Indicators	
Locates and uses a variety of primary and secondary sources	
Organizes and paraphrases relevant information from multiple sources into major categories	
Cites references/constructs bibliography using standard style	
Successful Learner Behaviors	
Responds appropriately to others, ideas, and feedback	
Uses cooperation and communication skills	
Exercises self-control	

Uses materials purposefully and respectfully	
Uses organizational strategies	
Actively listens, follows directions	
Stays on task, completes tasks on time	
Strives to produce quality work	

Class: **Integrated Algebra 6**

Teacher:

Number Sense and Computation Standards/Indicators	
Understands and uses whole numbers, fractions, decimals, integers	
Knows and uses basic facts efficiently	
Uses a variety of methods to estimate quantities	
Explains and performs computations in a variety of situations	
Knows and uses problem-solving strategies	
Learns and uses vocabulary related to math concepts	
Algebra, Patterns, and Functions Standards/Indicators	
Recognizes, extends, and creates patterns (all types)	
Uses symbols to solve equations	
Finds values and determines the rule for functions, input/output, t-tables (addition, subtraction, multiplication, division)	
Knows and uses problem-solving strategies	
Learns and uses vocabulary related to math concepts	
Statistics, Data, and Probability Standards/Indicators	
Uses probability to make predictions and designs	
Collects, organizes, displays, and interprets data	
Performs statistical measures on data (mean, median, mode, range)	
Knows and uses problem-solving strategies	
Learns and uses vocabulary related to math concepts	
Geometry and Measurement Standards/Indicators	
Recognizes, applies, and compares the properties of geometric shapes (classifies angles, triangles, etc.)	
Applies measurement strategies and formulas	
Performs measurement conversions in a variety of situations	
Recognizes, describes, and performs transformations (reflection, rotation, translation)	
Plots ordered pairs on a coordinate grid	
Knows and uses problem-solving strategies	
Learns and uses vocabulary related to math concepts	

Successful Learner Behaviors	
Responds appropriately to others, ideas, and feedback	
Uses cooperation and communication skills	
Exercises self-control	
Uses materials purposefully and respectfully	
Uses organizational strategies	
Actively listens, follows directions	
Stays on task, completes tasks on time	
Strives to produce quality work	

Class: **Orchestra 6**

Teacher:

Orchestra Standards/Indicators	
Performs on instrument with good posture, good playing position, and bow control	
Demonstrates appropriate tone while playing in an ensemble setting	
Uses instrumental techniques required for expressive performance of easy instrumental literature with simple keys, meters, and rhythms, within a limited range	
Creates and notates a short musical phrase using standard notation	
Reads and performs on his/her selected instrument whole, half, quarter, eighth, and dotted notes and corresponding rests in 2/4, 4/4, and 3/4 meter signatures	
Performs standard notation symbols	
Uses specific criteria to evaluate his/her and others' performance	
Identifies selected repertoire by genre, style, historical period, and/or composer	
Successful Learner Behaviors	
Responds appropriately to others, ideas, and feedback	
Uses cooperation and communication skills	
Exercises self-control	
Uses materials purposefully and respectfully	
Uses organizational strategies	
Actively listens, follows directions	
Stays on task, completes tasks on time	
Strives to produce quality work	

Class: **PHYSICAL EDUCATION 6**

Teacher:

Physical Education Standards/Indicators	
Demonstrates competency in motor skills and movement patterns needed to perform a variety of physical activities	
Demonstrates and understands movement concepts as they apply to the learning and performance of physical activities	
Achieves and maintains a health-enhancing level of physical fitness	
Successful Learner Behaviors	
Responds appropriately to others, ideas, and feedback	
Uses cooperation and communication skills	
Exercises self-control	
Uses materials purposefully and respectfully	
Uses organizational strategies	
Actively listens, follows directions	
Stays on task, completes tasks on time	
Strives to produce quality work	

Class: **Science 6**

Teacher:

Science Standards/Indicators	
Makes observations and applies scientific process skills	
Designs and conducts a scientific inquiry	
Uses tools and technology effectively	
Formulates decisions based on collection of data	
Learns and communicates using science vocabulary	
Learns concepts related to specific science content	
Understands effective strategies for personal safety	
Successful Learner Behaviors	
Responds appropriately to others, ideas, and feedback	
Uses cooperation and communication skills	
Exercises self-control	
Uses materials purposefully and respectfully	
Uses organization strategies	
Actively listens, follows directions	
Stays on task, completes tasks on time	
Strives to produce quality work	

Class: **Social Studies 6**

Teacher:

Social Studies Standards/Indicators	
Understands basic principles of government	
Understands basic economic concepts	
Formulates decisions based on historical concepts	
Uses five themes of geography (location, place, human interaction, region, movement)	
Understands and analyzes history through research	
Learns and communicates using social studies–related vocabulary	
Learns concepts related to specific social studies content	
Successful Learner Behaviors	
Responds appropriately to others, ideas, and feedback	
Uses cooperation and communication skills	
Exercises self-control	
Uses materials purposefully and respectfully	
Uses organizational strategies	
Actively listens, follows directions	
Stays on task, completes tasks on time	
Strives to produce quality work	

Grade Mark Legend	
S	Successfully meets: Meets academic (or learner behavior) expectations. Evidence of most recent work demonstrates that the learning goals are fully and consistently met.
M	Making progress: Partially meets academic (or learner behavior) expectations. Evidence of most recent work demonstrates more than half of the learning goals are fully and consistently met.
T	Targeted for growth in order to meet academic (or learner behavior) expectations. Evidence of most recent work demonstrates only a few of the learning goals are met or partially met.
E	Excels: Consistently goes beyond academic (or learner behavior) expectations. Evidence of most recent work demonstrates that the learning goals are fully and consistently met.
I	Incomplete: Insufficient evidence to report achievement.
S*	Successfully meets academic (or learner behavior) expectations with work modified and/or additional support provided (teacher, resource staff, etc.).
M*	Making progress: Partially meets academic (or learner behavior) expectations with work modified and/or additional support provided (teacher, resource staff, etc.).
T*	Targeted for growth in order to meet academic (or learner behavior) expectations with work modified and/or additional support provided (teacher, resource staff, etc.).
E*	Excels: Consistently goes beyond academic (or learner behavior) expectations with work modified and/or additional support provided (teacher, resource staff, etc.).
	Blank space: Standard not assessed during the quarter

* Additional support provided (teacher, para-educator, etc.)

Grade Mark Legend	
A	Meets and consistently goes beyond quarterly academic expectations. Almost all of the learning goals are fully or consistently met. This might be scores or most recent work of 90 or above.
B	Meets and may go beyond quarterly academic expectations. Most of the learning goals are fully or consistently met. This might be scores or more recent work of 80–89.
C	Meets quarterly academic expectations. Only a few of the learning goals are partially met. This might be scores or recent work of 70–79.
D	Partially meets quarterly academic expectations. Only a few of the learning goals are partially met. This might be scores or recent work of 60–69.
F	Does not meet quarterly academic expectations. None or almost none of the learning goals are met. This might be scores or most recent work of less than 60.

Source: Lawrence Public Schools, Lawrence, Kansas. Used with permission.

REFERENCES AND RESOURCES

Assessment Reform Group. (2002). *Assessment for learning: 10 research-based principles to guide classroom practice.* Accessed at http://arrts.gtcni.org.uk/gtcni/bitstream/2428/4623/1/Assessment%20 for%20Learning%20-%2010%20principles.pdf on November 12, 2011.

Association for Supervision and Curriculum Development (2012). *Educational Leadership, 70* (1), 11–78.

Atkin, J. M., Black, P., & Coffey, J. (Eds.). (2001). *Classroom assessment and the National Science Education Standards.* Washington, DC: National Academies Press.

Bailey, J. & Guskey, T. R. (2001). *Implementing student-led conferences.* Thousand Oaks, CA: Corwin Press.

Bailey, J., & McTighe, J. (1996). Reporting achievement at the secondary school level: What and how? In T. R. Guskey (Ed.), *Communicating student learning: ASCD Yearbook 1996* (pp. 119–140). Alexandria, VA: Association for Supervision and Curriculum Development.

Bangert-Downs, R. L., Kulik, C.-L. C., Kulik, J. A., & Morgan, M. T. (1991). The instructional effect of feedback in test-like events. *Review of Education Research, 61*(2), 213–238.

Bay District Schools. (2010). *Classroom assessment guiding principles.* Panama City, FL: Bay District Schools, Office of Assessment and Accountability.

Bloom, B. (1984). The search for methods of group instruction as effective as one-to-one tutoring. *Educational Leadership, 41*(8), 4–17.

Brookhart, S. M. (2009). *Grading* (2nd ed.). Upper Saddle River, NJ: Merrill.

Brookhart, S. M. (2011). Starting the conversation about grading. *Educational Leadership, 69*(3), 10–14.

Brown, A. L. (1994). The advancement of learning. *Educational Researcher, 23*(8), 4–12.

Brown, J. (2004). Grade-A perfect. *Principal Leadership, 5*(2), 28–32.

Burns, M. (2000). *About teaching mathematics: A K–8 resource* (2nd ed.). Sausalito, CA: Math Solutions.

Butler, R. (1987). Task-involving and ego-involving properties of evaluation: Effects of different feedback conditions on motivational perceptions, interest, and performance. *Journal of Educational Psychology, 79*(4), 474–482.

Chandler, M. A. (2012, January 15). In schools, self-esteem boosting is losing favor to rigor, finer-tuned praise. *Washington Post.* Accessed at www.washingtonpost.com/local/education/in-schools -self-esteem-boosting-is-losing-favor-to-rigor-finer-tuned-praise/2012/01/11/gIQAXFnF1P_story .html on January 16, 2012.

Chappuis, J. (2005). Helping students understand assessment. *Educational Leadership, 63*(3), 39–43.

Chappuis, J. (2009). *Seven strategies of assessment for learning.* Portland, OR: Educational Testing Service.

Chappuis, J., Stiggins, R. J., Chappuis, S., & Arter, J. A. (2012). *Classroom assessment for student learning: Doing it right—using it well* (2nd ed.). Upper Saddle River, NJ: Pearson.

Common Core State Standards Initiative. (2012). *Mathematics: Grade 5: Introduction.* Accessed at www .corestandards.org/the-standards/mathematics/grade-5/introduction on February 15, 2012.

Cooper, D. (2011). *Redefining fair: How to plan, assess, and grade for excellence in mixed-ability classrooms.* Bloomington, IN: Solution Tree Press.

Costa, A. L., & Kallick, B. (Eds.). (2000). *Discovering and exploring habits of mind.* Alexandria, VA: Association for Supervision and Curriculum Development.

Department of Education and Early Childhood Development. (2009). *Principles of learning and teaching P–12 and their components.* Accessed at www.education.vic.gov.au/studentlearning/teaching principles/principles/principlesandcomponents.htm on November 21, 2011.

Des Moines Public Schools. (n.d.a). *Policies and procedures.* Accessed at www.dmschools.org/board /administrative-policies-and-procedures/ on February 14, 2012.

Des Moines Public Schools. (n.d.b). *Series 600—Educational programs.* Accessed at www.dmschools.org /board/administrative-policies-and-procedures/series-600/ on February 12, 2012.

DuFour, R., & Marzano, R. J. (2011). *Leaders of learning: How district, school, and classroom leaders improve student achievement.* Bloomington, IN: Solution Tree Press.

Dweck, C. S. (2006). *Mindset: The new psychology of success.* New York: Random House.

El Monte City School District. (n.d.). *Parent guide to standards-based grading and reporting.* El Monte, CA: Author. Accessed at www.emcsd.org/sites/default/files/attachments/Standards%20Based%20 Reportcard%20Info.pdf on February 13, 2012.

Friedman, S. J. (1998). Grading teachers' grading policies. *National Association of Secondary Schools Bulletin, 82*(597), 77–83,

Goodreads. (n.d.). *Anaïs Nin quotations.* Accessed at www.goodreads.com/author/quotes/7190.Ana_s _Nin on July 3, 2012.

Guskey, T. R. (1996). Reporting on student learning: Lessons from the past-prescriptions for the future. In T. R. Guskey (Ed.), *Communicating student learning: ASCD Yearbook 1996* (pp. 13–24). Alexandria, VA: Association for Supervision and Curriculum Development.

Guskey, T. R. (2004). The communication challenge of standards-based reporting. *Phi Delta Kappan, 86*(4), 326–329.

Guskey, T. R., & Bailey, J. M. (2010). *Developing standards-based report cards.* Thousand Oaks, CA: Corwin Press.

Guskey, T. R., Swan, G. M., & Jung, L. A. (2011). Grades that mean something: Kentucky develops standards-based report cards. *Phi Delta Kappan, 93*(2), 52–57.

Habits of Mind. (n.d.). *Habits of mind word list.* Accessed at www.habitsofmind.org/content/habit-mind -word-list on September 12, 2012.

Hubbell Elementary School. (2010). *Hubbell Elementary assessment policy.* Accessed at http://old.dmps .k12.ia.us/schools/1Hubbell/docs/IB/Important%20Documents/Hubbell%20Assessment%20 Policy.pdf on February 12, 2012.

Kagan, S. (1995). Group grades miss the mark. *Educational Leadership, 52*(8), 68–71.

Kagan, S. (2000). Group grades are pointless. *Kagan Online Magazine.* Accessed at www.kaganonline .com/free_articles/dr_spencer_kagan/269/Group-Grades-Are-Pointless on February 24, 2012.

Kendall, J. S., & Marzano, R. J. (1997). *Content knowledge: A compendium of standards and benchmarks for K–12 education* (2nd ed.). Aurora, CO: McREL.

Kohn, A. (2011). The case against grades. *Educational Leadership, 69*(3), 28–33.

Lawrence Public Schools. (n.d.). Teaching and Learning. Accessed at www2.usd497.org/teachingand learning/progressreports/index.php

Lexington County School District One. (n.d.). Lexington One mission and vision. Accessed at www.lexington1 .net/lexoneweb/MissionVision.aspx on September 18, 2012.

Marshall, M. (2007). *Discipline without stress, punishments, or rewards: How teachers and parents promote responsibility & learning* (2nd ed.). Los Alamitos, CA: Piper Press.

Marshall, M. (2012). *Promoting responsibility & learning.* Accessed at http://MarvinMarshall.com on January 14, 2012.

Marzano, R. J., & Kendall, J. S. (1996). *A comprehensive guide to designing standards-based districts, schools, and classrooms.* Aurora, CO: McREL.

McTighe, J. (1997). What happens between assessments? *Educational Leadership, 54*(4), 6–12.

Millar-Grant, J., Heffler, B., & Mereweather, K. (1995). *Student-led conferences: Using portfolios to share learning with parents.* Markham, ON, Canada: Pembroke.

National Association of Elementary School Principals. (2002). *Leading learning communities: Standards for what principals should know and be able to do* (2nd ed.). Alexandria, VA: Author.

National Governors Association Center for Best Practices, & Council of Chief State School Officers. (2010). *Common core state standards.* Washington, DC: Authors.

North Central Regional Educational Laboratory. (n.d.a). *Criterion-referenced.* Accessed at www.ncrel.org /sdrs/areas/issues/methods/assment/as8lk3.htm on February 25, 2012.

North Central Regional Educational Laboratory. (n.d.b). *Norm-referenced.* Accessed at www.ncrel.org /sdrs/areas/issues/methods/assment/as8lk1.htm on February 25, 2012.

O'Connor, K. (2009). *How to grade for learning, K–12* (3rd ed.). Thousand Oaks, CA: Corwin Press.

O'Connor, K. (2011). *A repair kit for grading: 15 fixes for broken grades* (2nd ed.). Boston: Pearson.

O'Connor, K. (2012). *Fifteen fixes for broken grades: A repair kit.* Toronto, ON: Pearson.

Oliver, B. (2011). Making the case for standards-based grading. *Just for the ASKing! 8*(1). Accessed at www.justaskpublications.com/jfta/2011_1_jfta.htm on February 24, 2012.

Ontario Ministry of Education. (2010). *Growing success: Assessment, evaluation and reporting in Ontario schools.* Toronto, ON: Queen's Printer of Ontario. Accessed at www.edu.gov.on.ca/eng/policy funding/growSuccess.pdf on November 11, 2011.

Partnership for 21st Century Skills. (2009). *P21 framework definitions.* Accessed at www.p21.org/storage /documents/P21_Framework_Definitions.pdf on February 23, 2012.

Partnership for 21st Century Skills. (2011). *Framework for 21st century learning.* Accessed at www.p21.org /overview; accessed on February 23, 2012.

Pink, D. H. (2009). *Drive: The surprising truth about what motivates us.* New York: Riverhead Books.

Quakertown Community School District. (n.d.). *Why standards-based grading?* Quakertown, PA: Author. Accessed at www.qcsd.org/213010222123447650/lib/213010222123447650/SBG_brochure.pdf on February 24, 2012.

Sadler, D. R. (1989). Formative assessment and the design of instructional systems. *Instructional Science, 18*(2), 119–144.

Stiggins, R. (1994). *Student-centered classroom assessment.* New York: Merrill.

Sullo, B. (2009). *The motivated student: Unlocking the enthusiasm for learning.* Alexandria, VA: Association for Supervision and Curriculum Development.

Tileston, D. W. (2004). *What every teacher should know about student motivation.* Thousand Oaks, CA: Corwin Press.

Tombari, M. L., & Borich, G. D. (1999). *Authentic assessment in the classroom: Applications and practice.* Upper Saddle River, NJ: Merrill/Prentice Hall.

Tyre, P. (2012). Making the grade: When do kids deserve A's? *Family Circle.* Accessed at www.familycircle .com/teen/school/homework/grades/? on January 20, 2012.

Washington Saratoga Warren Hamilton Essex BOCES. (n.d.). *Homework Decision Tree.* New York: Author.

Wiggins, G., & McTighe, J. (2005). *Understanding by design* (expanded 2nd ed.). Alexandria, VA: Association for Supervision and Curriculum Development.

Wikipedia. (2011). *Principle.* Accessed at http://en.wikipedia.org/wiki/Principle on November 11, 2011.

Wiliam, D. (2011). *Embedded formative assessment.* Bloomington, IN: Solution Tree Press.

Willis, J. (2006). *Research-based strategies to ignite student learning: Insights from a neurologist and class-room teacher.* Alexandria, VA: Association for Supervision and Curriculum Development.

INDEX

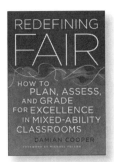

Redefining Fair
Damian Cooper
Learn how to define proficiency accurately and differentiate to help all students achieve it. Using stories, strategies, case histories, and sample documents, the author explains how to implement equitable instruction, assessment, grading, and reporting practices for diverse 21st century learners.
BKF412

Elements of Grading
Douglas B. Reeves
Learn several strategies for improving grading practices, while examining the common arguments against reform. With this practical guide, you can improve grading to meet four essential criteria—accuracy, fairness, specificity, and timeliness—and also make the process quicker and more efficient.
BKF410

Ahead of the Curve
Edited by Douglas B. Reeves
Get the anthology that offers the ideas and recommendations of many of the world's leaders in assessment. Many perspectives on effective assessment design and implementation culminate in a call for redirecting assessment to improve student achievement and inform instruction.
BKF232

Grading and Learning
Susan M. Brookhart
Grades should reflect and motivate learning. This book is relatable, relevant, and effective in improving educators' assessment and reporting processes and supporting students' motivation to learn. Clear, concrete examples help translate state standards into curriculum goals.
BKF457

Embedded Formative Assessment
Dylan Wiliam
Emphasizing the instructional side of formative assessment, this book explores in-depth the use of classroom questioning, learning intentions and success criteria, feedback, collaborative and cooperative learning, and self-regulated learning to engineer effective learning environments for students.
BKF418

Solution Tree | Press   a division of
Solution Tree

Visit solution-tree.com or call 800.733.6786 to order.

Solution Tree

Solution Tree's mission is to advance the work of our authors. By working with the best researchers and educators worldwide, we strive to be the premier provider of innovative publishing, in-demand events, and inspired professional development designed to transform education to ensure that all students learn.

The mission of the National Association of Elementary School Principals is to lead in the advocacy and support for elementary and middle level principals and other education leaders in their commitment for all children.